Easy and Fun Ways to Learn Spanish for Beginners at Home, Office or in Your Car

How to Understand and Speak a New language in 15 Days.
Contains Spanish Grammar, Phrases, Exercises and Pronunciation

Francisco Ruiz

Table of Contents

Disclaimer

Copyright

INTRODUCTION

Welcome to the book for Learning for Spanish beginners. The exercises included here are designed to help develop your reading and writing skills in Spanish while you practice the vocabulary and grammar presented in the lessons. This introduction briefly explains how this book fits in with the other components that accompany this course so that you'll know how best to make use of all of them to help develop your Spanish skills.

Each section of this book begins with New Vocabulary,the General Review section summarizes the material covered in the lesson, allowing you to review grammatical, cultural, or vocabulary-related content. Then, you will find the Activities, which offer practice with the new grammar and vocabulary. At the end of every workbook section, you will find the Correct Answers, which will allow you to check your work. In addition to the Activities included after every lesson, this book also contains six Cultural Readings about different aspects of Latin American culture.

The Activities in this book are contextualized in a series of short stories dealing with several families and their friends and neighbors. These families live in Villa Celeste [Celestial Town], a neighborhood somewhere in Latin America. The principal characters in the stories are the Cortés Ruiz family, the Quirós García family, and the González Fallas family. The Cortés Ruiz family has three sons, and the Quirós

García family has two daughters and a son. Those two families also have two very young granddaughters. The González Fallas family, who just recently moved to the neighborhood, has a son and a daughter. You will find the family trees for these families following this introduction.

Most of the words used in the Activities will be ones you will have already been introduced to in the course. When this is not the case, the book will give the English for the Spanish word. The six Cultural Readings do indeed include vocabulary and grammar you will have already seen in the course. But they also purposely include some material a bit beyond your current level of comprehension. This will force you to make some educated guesses while reading—a very useful skill for a language learner. You won't need to recognize every word or expression in a reading to gain a good understanding of it. The English translation for the Cultural Readings can be found after the Correct Answers, so you will be able to see how well your understood what you read.

And now, it's time to get to work. Or, as we would say in Spanish: **A trabajar!** [Let's work!].

Introduction to the Spanish Language

I. Vocabulario nuevo / New Vocabulary

hola – hello **Qué tal?** – How's it going? **Cómo estás?** – How are you? [informal, singular]	**Cómo está usted?** – How are you? [formal, singular] **Cómo están ustedes?** – How are you? [formal, plural]
Bien, gracias. ¿Y tú? – Fine, thanks. And you? [informal, singular]	**Bien, gracias. ¿Y ustedes?** – Fine, thanks. And you? [formal, plural]
bien – well **Estoy bien.** – I'm well. **mal** – not well **Estoy mal.** – I'm not well	**regular** – so-so **más o menos** – so-so **no muy bien** – not very well
Buenos días–good morning **buen día** – good morning	**buenas tardes** – good afternoon **buenas noches** – good evening, good night
Me llamo…. – My name is…. **Soy….** – I am…. **Mi nombre es….** – My name is…. **mucho gusto** – nice to meet you	**Cómo te llamas?** – What's your name? [informal, singular] **Cómo se llama usted?** – What's your name? [formal, singular]
encantado – pleased to meet you [speaker masculine] **igualmente** – likewise	**Es un placer.** – It's a pleasure **encantada** – pleased to meet you [speaker feminine]
gracias – thank you **muy** – very	**muy bien, gracias** – very well, thank you **bastante bien** – just fine
bienvenidos – welcome [plural] **Te presento a….** – Let me	**Le presento a….** – Let me introduce you to…. [formal,

introduce you to…. [informal, singular]	singular]
adiós – good-bye **chao** – bye **hasta luego** – see you later	**hasta mañana** – see you tomorrow **hasta pronto** – see you soon **nos vemos** – see you
el curso – course **los Estados Unidos** – United States **el aspecto** – aspect	**la lengua** – language **el español** – Spanish language **el castellano** – Spanish language **la cultura** – culture
introductorio – introductory **importante** – important	**solo** – alone, only

Repaso general / General Review

Approach to Learning a New Language

Successful language learners have a positive reaction when faced with the unfamiliar. So, rather than allowing yourself to feel frustrated, confused, or annoyed when listening to Spanish, try to maintain a positive outlook and work to understand anything you can. It can help to think of communicating in Spanish as a puzzle to be solved or an interesting challenge to be met. When you hear spoken Spanish, focus on what's being said, don't be distracted by negative thoughts, and listen for cognates, which are words that are the same or almost the same in two languages. Spanish and English share many cognates, including curso / course; introductorio / introductory; profesor / professor; importante / important; aspecto / aspect; cultura / culture; and mucho / much.

The Spanish Language

The Spanish language, known as either español or castellano, developed in the Iberian Peninsula in the region of Castile, or Castilla in Spanish. According to the United Nations, Spanish is the third most-spoken language in the world, after Mandarin Chinese and English. Roughly half a billion people speak Spanish, which is spoken on four continents, is an official language of 20 countries, and is one of the official languages (along with English) of the U.S. territory of Puerto Rico. Spanish is also spoken more and more each year in the mainland United States. According to the latest census data, almost 40 million people in the United States speak Spanish at home, which makes up more than 12 percent of the country's population. A 2015 report by the Instituto Cervantes, a governmental organization in Spain that focuses on the Spanish language, concluded that there are more Spanish speakers in the United States than there are in Spain.

Varieties of Spoken Spanish

The three main differences that distinguish how Spanish is spoken in one place versus another are vocabulary, accent, and grammar. Differences in vocabulary result in different words being used in different places to refer to the same thing. To say "the computer," for example, in Latin America you'd say la computadora, while in Spain it's much more common to say el ordenador.

In terms of accent, there are differences between countries and even between regions within the same country. Perhaps the most notable difference in accent among Spanish speakers relates to the way to pronounce the letter **z** and the letter **c** followed by **e** or **i.** In Latin America, the letter **z** and the letter combinations **ce** and **ci** are pronounced with an **s** sound, while in northern and central Spain this is pronounced with a th sound. The Spanish word for "shoe" is **zapato**, which in Madrid is pronounced as "**th**apato" and in Latin America is pronounced "sapato."

There are not many grammatical differences among regions, but there are a few, and one deals with the plural form of "you." In both Spain and Latin America, the word ustedes is the formal, plural way to say "you." In Spain, there's also an informal, plural way to say "you," which is vosotros in the masculine or vosotras in the feminine. But vosotros and vosotras are not used in Latin America; instead, ustedes is used for the plural "you" in all cases.

Despite these differences in vocabulary, accent, and grammar, hundreds of millions of Spanish speakers communicate successfully across all the countries where the language is spoken. Speakers of Spanish—even from different regions—understand each other extremely well.

Pronunciation of Vowels

Pronouncing words in Spanish is simpler than it is in English because when you look at a letter in Spanish, with very rare exceptions you know exactly how to pronounce the sound of that letter. One challenging aspect of Spanish

pronunciation is that there are sounds in the language that don't exist in English, and these can be difficult to pronounce at first.

Each of the five vowels—a, e, i, o, u—makes just one sound in Spanish, a short sound that stays the same from beginning to end.

• A, found in the common Spanish word casa, is the easiest vowel sound to make. For the other four vowel sounds, focus on keeping the vowel sound short and uniform.

• E makes the sound pronounced in the English word "take." It's not "eyyyy." You don't close it off at the end as

you often do in English.

• I makes the sound pronounced in the word "fee." It's not "iyyyy."

• O makes the sound pronounced in "toll." It's not "owwww."

• U makes the sound pronounced in "rule." It's not "uwwww."

The video lessons, audio glossaries, and speaking activities model proper pronunciation in Spanish.

Greetings

Among the very common greetings in Spanish are hola [h

tal? [How's it going?]; and ¿Cómo estás? and ¿Cómo está usted? [How are you?]. ¿Cómo estás? is the informal way to say "How are you?" to someone. ¿Cómo está usted? also asks "How are you?" but is used with someone you address formally.

Three ways to introduce yourself are Me llamo Bill [I call myself Bill, or My name is Bill]; Soy Bill [I am Bill]; and Mi nombre es Bill [My name is Bill].

Common expressions used when you meet someone for the first time are mucho gusto [nice to meet you]; encantado [pleased to meet you, masculine form]; encantada [pleased to meet you, feminine form]; Es un placer [It's a pleasure]; and igualmente [likewise].

Greetings dependent on the time of day include buenos días or buen día [good morning]; buenas tardes [good afternoon]; and buenas noches [good evening, or good night]. Ways to say "goodbye" include adiós [goodbye]; chao [bye]; hasta luego [see you later]; hasta mañana [see you tomorrow]; hasta pronto [see you soon]; and nos vemos [see you].

How Best to Approach This Course

If your goal is to work toward proficiency in Spanish, you should watch the video lessons and engage with the other course materials as well. In order to make significant progress with your language skills, you'll need to practice what's presented in the video lessons.

When you finish a lesson, you should next listen to the audio glossary, which will give you the pronunciation and definition of all new vocabulary words. Then, it will be time to practice what you've learned. The speaking activities for each lesson are designed to help you improve your listening and speaking skills. And the workbook exercises will allow you to practice your reading and writing. You can decide if you want to do the speaking activities before or after you do the workbook exercises, but you should do both of these only after watching the video lesson and listening to the audio glossary.

If you are able to involve someone else with your studies, you are encouraged to do so. Languages are meant for social interaction, so take the course with a friend or seek out opportunities to speak Spanish with someone who already knows the language. The more contact you have with Spanish, both within the course and beyond it, the better your progress will be.

Global Importance of the Spanish Language

Although it might seem that Spanish has gained importance in the United States only recently, in 1787 Thomas Jefferson wrote the following about the Spanish language in a letter to his nephew: "Bestow great attention on this, and endeavor to acquire an accurate knowledge of it. Our future connections with Spain and Spanish

America, will render that language a valuable acquisition." What was true in Jefferson's time remains true today. Spanish is a world language, and its importance now extends beyond its use in other countries to the mainland of the United States.

Acquiring Spanish is a way of broadening your horizons and becoming more connected to the diverse traditions that are being lived out across oceans and right next door. A sincere desire to learn accompanied by diligent practice makes acquiring Spanish an achievable goal for people of all ages. And the benefits of being able to communicate in Spanish are significant. After all, half a billion people are waiting to talk with you.

Actividades / Activities

Carlos González y Alejandra Fallas se acaban de mudar con su familia al vecindario Villa Celeste y están saludando y conociendo a sus vecinos. / Carlos González and Alejandra Fallas have just moved with their family to the neighborhood Villa Celeste and are greeting and getting to know their neighbors.

a. Completa las siguientes frases con la expresión apropiada. / Complete the following sentences with the appropriate expression.

1. Esteban: Hola, ¿_____ están?

2. Carlos: ¡_____, gracias!

3. Esteban: ¿Cómo _____?

4. Carlos: _____ Carlos. ¿Y usted?

5. Esteban: _____ Esteban, y ella es mi esposa [and she is my wife], Luisa.

6. Carlos: ¡_____ gusto! Ella es mi esposa, Alejandra.

7. Alejandra: ¡_____!

8. Luisa: ¡_____!

b. Escribe una expresión similar a la expresión original. / Write an expression similar to the original expression.

1. Encantado. _____

2. ¿Qué tal? _____

3. Muy bien, gracias. _____

4. Más o menos. _____

5. Mi nombre es.... _ _____

6. Nos vemos. _____

c. Escoge una respuesta apropiada en cada situación. / Choose an appropriate answer in each situation.

1. Hola. ¿Cómo está?

a) Igualmente. b) Bien, gracias. ¿Y usted? c) Hasta luego.

2. Le presento a Luisa.

a) Más o menos. b) Bien, gracias. c) Mucho gusto.

3. Buenas tardes. ¿Qué tal?

a) Igualmente. b) Muy bien. ¿Y usted? c) Nos vemos.

4. Hasta mañana.

a) Regular. b) Encantado. c) Hasta pronto.

5. ¿Cómo te llamas?

a) Igualmente. b) Buenos días. c) Me llamo Carlos.

6. ¡Buenas noches! ¿Cómo estás?

a) Bien, gracias. ¿Y tú? b) ¿Y usted? c) Encantada.

d. Agrega la expresión apropiada. / Add the appropriate expression.

1. ¡Buenas   a. está usted?

2. ¿Cómo te   b. tal?

3. ¿Qué   c. gusto!

4. ¡Mucho   d. Carlos

5. Les   e. presento a mi amigo.

6. ¡Hasta   f. llamas?

7. ¿Cómo   g. pronto!

8. Mi nombre es h. tardes!

IV. Respuestas correctas / Correct Answers

a. 1. ¿Cómo están?

2. ¡Bien, gracias! / ¡Muy bien, gracias!

3. ¿Cómo se llama usted?

4. Me llamo Carlos / Soy Carlos / Mi nombre es Carlos.

5. Soy Esteban / Mi nombre es Esteban / Me llamo Esteban.

6. ¡Mucho gusto!

7. ¡Mucho gusto! / ¡Encantada! / ¡Es un placer!

8. ¡Igualmente!

b. 1. Mucho gusto. / Igualmente. / Es un placer.

2. ¿Cómo está usted? / ¿Cómo estás?

3. Bien, gracias..

4. Regular

5. Soy…. / Me llamo

6. Hasta luego. / Hasta pronto. / Adiós. / Chao.

c. 1. b) Bien, gracias. ¿Y usted?

2. c) Mucho gusto.

3. b) Muy bien. ¿Y usted?

4. c) Hasta pronto.

5. c) Me llamo Carlos.

6. a) Bien, gracias. ¿Y tú?

d. 1. h) ¡Buenas tardes!

2. f) ¿Cómo te llamas?

3. b) ¿Qué tal?

4. c) ¡Mucho gusto!

5. e) Les presento a mi amigo.

6. g) ¡Hasta pronto!

7. a) ¿Cómo está usted?

8. d) Mi nombre es Carlos.

Definite Articles and Nouns

Vocabulario nuevo / New Vocabulary

el – the [masculine, singlar] **la** – the [feminine, singular]	**los** – the [masculine, plural] **las** – the [feminine, plural]
el libro – book **la silla** – chair **la mesa** – table **la casa** – house **la clase** – class **el reloj** – watch, clock **el lápiz** – pencil **la pared** – wall **la música** – music **el televisor** – television set **el papel** – paper	**la mano** – hand **el mapa** – map **el problema** – problem **el sistema** – system **el día** – day **el cuaderno** – notebook, workbook **el agua** – water [feminine] **la letra** – letter **el hotel** – hotel **la familia** – family
interesante – interesting **popular** – popular **inteligente** – intelligent	**clásico** – classical **central** – central
la educación – education **la nación** – nation **la lección** – lesson **la universidad** – university	**la libertad** – liberty, freedom **la posibilidad** – possibility **la actitud** – attitude **la virtud** – virtue
el pianista – male pianist **la pianista** – female pianist **el dentista** – male dentist **la dentista** – female dentist **el futbolista** – male soccer player **la futbolista** – female soccer player **el chico** – boy	**el señor** – Mr., man **la señora** – Mrs., woman **la señorita** – Miss, young woman **el profesor** – male professor **la profesora** – female professor **el doctor** – male doctor **la doctora** – female doctor **llamar** – to call

la chica – girl	
en – in **de** – of, from	**hay** – there is, there are
el norte – north **el oeste** – west	**el sur** – south **el este** – east

Repaso general / General Review

Geography of the Spanish-Speaking World

Spanish is spoken in Europe, North America, Central America, the Caribbean, South America, and Africa. The countries where Spanish is spoken as an official language within each of these regions are as follows.

• Europe: Spain.

• North America: Mexico.

• Central America: Guatemala, El Salvador, Honduras, Nicaragua, Costa Rica, Panama. •• The Caribbean: Cuba, the Dominican Republic, Puerto Rico.

• South America: Venezuela, Colombia, Ecuador, Peru, Bolivia, Paraguay, Chile, Uruguay, Argentina.

• Africa: Equatorial Guinea.

As you learned in the first lesson, the United States has more Spanish speakers than Spain; in fact, the United States has more Spanish speakers than any other country except Mexico. Spanish is also widely spoken in Canada, Belize, and the Philippines.

Nouns

All nouns in Spanish have a gender, meaning that they are either masculine or feminine. Most nouns that end in -o are masculine, while most that end in -a are feminine. Beyond gender, nouns also have a number, meaning that they are either singular or plural.

Definite Articles

While "the" is the only definite article in English, in Spanish there are four forms of the definite article: el (masculine singular), la (feminine singular), los (masculine plural), and las (feminine plural). Examples of definite articles used with nouns include el libro [the book]; la mesa [the table]; los cuadernos [the notebooks, or the workbooks]; las señoras [the women]. When the preposition de [of] is followed by the definite article el, de + el contracts to del. So, El cuaderno del curso is "The workbook of the course," or "The course's workbook."

Although nouns ending in -o are usually masculine and nouns ending in -a are usually feminine, there are many nouns in Spanish that have an ending other than -o or -a. For that reason, you should always learn a new noun with its accompanying definite article. As you learn, for example, that "the hotel" is el hotel, you are reinforcing that hotel is a masculine noun. And you need to know the gender of a noun, for example, so that you can use the proper form of an adjective to describe the noun.

Definite articles have a variety of uses in Spanish. As is the case with English, they can refer to something specific. For example, "The class is interesting" is La clase es interesante. Unlike English, definite articles are also used when talking about a noun in a general sense. To say, for example, "Freedom is important," you would say La libertad es importante. Definite articles are also needed when speaking or writing about people with titles, such as señor, señora, señorita, profesor, profesora, doctor, and doctora. To say "Professor Ana Cano is popular," for example, you would say La profesora Ana Cano es popular. No definite article is needed when talking directly to a person with a title, so "Hello, Professor Cano" is Hola, Profesora Cano.

Knowing the Gender of a Noun

You have learned that nouns ending in -a are usually feminine. Words ending in the suffixes -ión, -ad, and -tud are also almost always feminine. Examples of feminine nouns with these suffixes include la lección [lesson], la posiblilidad [possibility], and la virtud [virtue]. [Note: Technically, la lección, for example, means "the lesson."

In the way that nouns ending in -o are usually masculine, nouns ending in -r and -l are also usually masculine. Examples of masculine nouns ending in -r and -l include el televisor [television set] and el hotel [hotel].

Words ending in -ista look feminine because they end in -a. But these words actually can be either masculine or feminine, as seen, for example, in el futbolista [male soccer player] and la futbolista [female soccer player]. Spanish words ending in -ma also look feminine because of the -a ending, but many of these words are actually masculine, including el sistema [system] and el problema [problem]. Specific words that seem to be one gender but are the other include el día [day] and el mapa [map], which are masculine, and la mano [hand], which is feminine. Feminine nouns beginning with the sound -a in a stressed syllable use el rather than la as their definite article. El agua [water], for example, is indeed a feminine noun, but it uses el rather than la as its definite article. [Note: If la were used as the definite article for agua, then the two a sounds when pronounced would run together and sound like laaaagua. Using el instead of la avoids this problem.] Feminine nouns beginning with the sound a in a syllable that is not stressed keep the usual definite article of la (e.g., la actitud [attitude]).

Making Nouns Plural

The three rules for making a noun plural in Spanish are as follows.

1. If a noun ends in a vowel, add **-s**: la silla [chair] à las sillas.

2. If a noun ends in a consonant other than **z**, add **-es**: el papel [paper] à los papeles

3. If a noun ends in a **z**, change the **z to c** and add **-es**: el lápiz [pencil] à los lápices

The Alphabet in Spanish

The Spanish alphabet has 27 letters. They include the 26 used in English plus the letter ñ (as seen in España), which comes right after the letter n in the alphabet.

Pronunciation of Several Consonant Sounds

Pronunciation is not about letters, and it's not about spelling—it's about sound. So, listen carefully when you hear words in Spanish and do your best to reproduce the sounds you hear.

The letters **f, l, m,** and **n** are pronounced the same in Spanish as they are in English and are found in such words as la **profesora** [female professor], la **libertad** [liberty, freedom], la **música** [music], and la **nación** [nation].

The letter **s** is always pronounced as s and never as **z**. The name José, for example, is pronounced with an **s** sound, not a **z** sound.

The letter **h** is silent in Spanish, so **el hotel** [hotel], for example, should be pronounced as **el otel**. When h follows **c**, it makes a ch sound, as found in la chica [girl].

The letter **t** in Spanish is never aspirated when pronounced, meaning that you produce no puff of air when you make the sound of **t**. In fact, the t in Spanish sounds like a combination of **t** and **d**.

The sound that corresponds with single **r** in Spanish is similar to the sound made when **d** is pronounced in English. The sound corresponding to **j** in Spanish, as used in the names Juan and José, has no exact equivalent in English. Both the audio glossaries and the speaking activities offer numerous opportunities for you to listen to the pronunciation of words in Spanish and practice your own pronunciation. The best way to improve your pronunciation is to listen carefully when you hear Spanish and speak a lot of Spanish yourself.

Actividades / Activities

a. Agrega el artículo definido apropiado a cada sustantivo. / Add the appropriate definite article to each noun.

1. _____ universidad

2. _____ libros

3. _____ día

4. _____ lápices

5. _____ Sistema

6. _____ cuadernos

7. _____ mapas

8. _____ educación

9. _____ actitud

b. La familia de González está descubriendo las razones que tienen las cosas necesarias en sus nuevos / The González Fallas family is unpacking the boxes that have the things needed in their new home.

Ayuda a la familia González Fallas a desempacar sus cosas. Agrega el artículo definido apropiado a cada sustantivo. / Help the González Fallas family unpack their things. Add the appropriate definite article to each noun.

1. _____ televisor

2. _____ mesas

3. _____ lámparas [lamps]

4. _____ papeles

5. _____ computadora [computer]

6. _____ alfombra [rug]

7. _____ cuadernos

8. _____ mapas

9. _____ libros

10. _____ mesas

c. La familia González Fallas no recuerda cuántas cosas tienen en las cajas. / The González Fallas family doesn't remember how many things they have in the boxes.

Ayúdalos haciendo el plural de las siguientes cosas que han desempacado. / Help them by making the plural of the following things they have unpacked.

1. el cuaderno _____

2. la lámpara _____

3. el televisor _____

4. el zapato [shoe] _____

5. el mapa _____

6. la alfombra _____

7. la cama [bed] _____

8. el reloj _____

9. la bicicleta [bicycle] _____

10. el perfume [perfume] _____

11. el papel _____

12. el lápiz _____

d. Escoge la respuesta correcta. / Choose the correct answer.

1. ¿Cuál [What] es el plural de reloj? *a) relojes b) relojs c) relojeces*

2. ¿Cuál es el singular de televisores*? a) televiso b) televisor c) televisore*

3. ¿Cuál es el plural de hotel? *a) hotel b) hoteles c) hotels*

4. ¿Cuál es el singular de doctoras? *a) doctor b) doctoras c) doctora*

5. ¿Cuál es el artículo definido de sistema? *a) la b) las c) el*

6. ¿Cuál es el artículo definido de mano? *a) el b) la c) los*

7. ¿Cuál es el artículo definido de problemas? *a) los b) las c) el*

8. ¿Cuál es el artículo definido de dentistas? *a) los b) las c) la*

9. ¿Cuál es el artículo definido de futbolistas? *a) los b) las c) la*

10. ¿Cuál es el artículo definido de papel? *a) la b) el c) las*

Respuestas correctas / Correct Answers

a. 1. la Universidad   4. los lápices   7. los mapas

2. los libros   5. el sistema   8. la educación

3. el día   6. los cuadernos   9. la actitud

b. 1. el   6. la

2. las   7. los

3. las   8. los

4. los   9. los

5. la   10. las

c. 1. los cuadernos   7. las camas

2. las lámparas   8. los relojes

3. los televisores   9. las bicicletas

4. los zapatos   10. los perfumes

5. los mapas   11. los papeles

6. las alfombras   12. los lápices

d. 1. a) relojes

2. b) televisor

3. b) hoteles

4. c) doctora

5 c) el

6. b) la

7. a) los

8. a) los and b) las

9. a) los and b) las

10. b) el

Subject Pronouns and the Verb Ser

Vocabulario nuevo / New Vocabulary

Yo – I **él** – he **ella** – she	**usted** – you [singular, formal] **tú** – you [singular, informal]
nosotros – we [masculine] **ustedes** – you [plural, formal] **nosotras** – we [feminine] **ellos** – they [masculine]	**vosotros** – you [masculine plural, informal] **ellas** – they [feminine] **vosotras** – you [feminine plural, informal]
ser – to be **¡Hablen!** – Speak! [pluralcommand]	**¡No esperen!** – Don't wait! [plural command]
alto – tall **accidental** – accidental **simpático** – nice **usual** – usual **antipático** – unfriendly **normal** – normal **guapo** – good-looking **optimista** – optimistic	**bonito** – pretty **pesimista** – pessimistic **feo** – ugly **activo** – active **joven** – young **responsable** – responsible **viejo** – old
largo – long **embarazada** – pregnant **corto** – short in length **elegante** – elegant **grande** – big **excelente** – excellent	**pequeño** – small **fantástico** – fantastic **avergonzado** – embarrassed
el accidente – accident **el taxi** – taxi **la cuestión** – question, issue	**la pregunta** – question **el colegio** – high school

el teléfono – telephone	
la persona – person el amigo – male friend el vecino – male neighbor la amiga – female friend la vecina – female neighbor el novio – boyfriend	el hombre – man la novia – girlfriend la mujer – woman
y – and sí – yes o – or no – no, not	pero – but ahora – now

Repaso general / General Review

Improving Your Ability to Speak

It's important as a beginning language learner that you take every opportunity to speak Spanish. Don't wait until you've learned more vocabulary and grammar. ¡Hablen español ahora! ["Speak Spanish now!"] The best way to improve your spoken Spanish is to speak more.

Subject Pronouns

The singular subject pronouns in Spanish are yo – I; tú – you [singular, informal]; usted – you [singular, formal]; él – he; and ella – she. The plural subject pronouns are **nosotros** – we [masculine]; nosotras – we [feminine]; vosotros – you [masculine plural, informal]; **vosotras** –

you [feminine plural, informal]; ustedes – you [plural, formal]; **ellos** – they [masculine]; and **ellas** – they [feminine].

The informal, singular way to say "you" is tú; the formal, singular way to say "you" is **usted**. If you're speaking to a family member, a friend, or someone else you're well acquainted with, you'll probably use tú. You'll use usted when talking with someone you have a formal relationship with or with someone you don't know well. If you're not sure which pronoun to use, it's better to use usted, because using the informal tú can be seen as rude by someone you don't know well.

The vosotros and vosotras forms, which are plural, informal ways to say "you," are used only in Spain. In Latin America, the plural of tú is ustedes and the plural of usted is ustedes; vosotros and vosotras are never used in Latin America.

The pronouns nosotros, vosotros, and ellos are used when referring to a group of all men or a mixed group of men and women. Even a group of many women and just one man would be referred to with these masculine pronouns. The pronouns nosotras, vosotras, and ellas are used only when every member of the group is female.

The Verb ser

The infinitive form, which is the verb form found in the dictionary, of all Spanish verbs ends in **-ar, -er**, or **-ir. Ser,** the infinitive form meaning "to be," has the following six forms in the present tense: **soy,**

eres, es, somos, sois, son. Conjugating a verb means giving its proper verb forms for different subjects in a given tense. **Ser** is conjugated with the subject pronouns in the present tense as follows.

Ser with singular subject pronouns:

yo soy; tú eres; usted, él, or ella es

Ser with plural subject pronouns:

nosotros or nosotras somos;

vosotros or vosotra

sois; ustedes, ellos, or ellas son

Any singular subject that is not yo or tú uses the verb form es (e.g., La clase es importante).

Any plural subject that is not nosotros, nosotras, vosotros, or vosotras uses the verb form son (e.g., **Los amigos son optimistas**).

Ser is used 1) to identify a person or thing (**Ella es Claudia**); 2) to talk about one's profession (**Son doctores**), origin, or nationality (**Roberto es de Chile**); or 3) to describe inherent characteristics of someone or something (**Carla es inteligente; El hotel es elegante.**).

Cognates

Spanish and English share many cognates, which are words that are the same or similar in two languages. Sometimes Spanish cognates are spelled the same as the word in English: **normal, hotel, usual**. Other Spanish cognates are spelled similar to, but not the same as, the word in English: **activo, responsable, excelente**. Your comprehension of Spanish will improve if you listen for cognates when conversing and look for them when reading.

Occasionally, a Spanish word will look like an English word but mean something else. These words are called false cognates. Examples include **largo** (which looks like "large" but means "long") and colegio (which looks like "college" but means "high school"). False cognates, however, are relatively rare compared to the vast number of cognates shared by English and Spanish.

Adjectives

Adjectives in Spanish must agree in number and gender with the noun being modified. So, if the subject is masculine singular, the adjective must also be masculine singular, and if the subject is feminine plural, the adjective must also be feminine plural.

Adjectives ending in -o have four forms. For example, **viejo**, meaning "old," has the following four forms: **viejo** (masculine singular); **vieja** (feminine singular); **viejos** (masculine plural); **viejas** (feminine plural).

Adjectives ending in -e have two forms, as can be seen in **responsable** (masculine and feminine singular) and **responsables** (masculine and feminine plural).

Adjectives ending in -ista have two forms, as can be seen in **pesimista** (masculine and feminine singular) and **pesimistas** (masculine and feminine plural).

Actividades / Activities

a. Dedíquese si debe dirigirse a las siguientes personas de manera o de manera informal. / Decide if you should address the following people in a formal or informal way.

1. You are about to call your friend to ask him to watch the game with you._____.

2. Your uncle wants to borrow your car._____

3. Your boss just sent you an email. _ _____

4. Your neighbor is inviting you to a gathering on Saturday._ _____

5. The CEO of the company is entering the room._____

6. You just met someone._____

7. The President of the United States is coming to your town. _ ___

8. You and your sister are going to celebrate her birthday. _____

9. Someone called and it was a wrong number. _ _____

10. You meet a random person at the supermarket._____

b. Alejandra está hablando sobre su familia con su vecina Cecilia. / Alejandra is talking about her family with her neighbor Cecilia.

Agrega la conjugación correcta del verbo ser. / Add the correct conjugation of the verb ser.

1. Carlos _____ mi esposo [my husband].

2. Pablo _____ mi hijo [son].

3. Marisol _____ mi hija [daughter].

4. Pablo y Marisol _____ mis hijos [children].

5. Yo _____ la esposa [wife] de Carlos.

6. Yo _____ la madre [mother] de Pablo y Marisol.

7. Nosotros _____ la familia González Fallas.

8. Carlos _____ el padre [father] de Pablo y Marisol.

9. ¿De dónde _____ usted y Luis?

c. La familia González Fallas continúa conociendo a los miembros de su nuevo vecindario en Villa Celeste. / The González Fallas family continues to meet the members of their new neighborhood in Villa Celeste.

Completa el diálogo entre Alejandra, Luisa, Pablo y Marisol usando el verbo **ser** y palabras para saludarse y presentarse. / Complete the dialogue between Alejandra, Luisa, Pablo, and Marisol using the verb ser and words to greet others and introduce oneself.

Alejandra: ¡Hola! Me 1) _____ Alejandra.

Luisa: Mucho 2) _____. 3)_____Luisa.

Alejandra: Le 4) _____ a Pablo. Él 5) _____ mi hijo.

Luisa: ¡Encantada! Mi nombre 6) _____ Luisa.

Pablo: 7) _____. Ella 8) _____ mi Hermana Marisol.

Marisol: ¿Qué tal?

Luisa: 9) ¡_____ bien, gracias!

Luisa: Le 10) _____ mi hijab Elena. Ella 11) _____ estudiante de la universidad.

Marisol: 12) ¡_____ gusto!

Elena: Igualmente. Erica y Felipe 13) _____ mis hermanos.

d. Elena está hablando con Marisol. / Elena is talking with Marisol.

¿Qué pronombres personales necesita Elena para hablar de…? / What subject pronouns does Elena need to talk about…?

1. Mis amigos y yo _____.

2. Mis vecinas _____.

3. El ex-novio [ex-boyfriend] de Elena _____.

4. Los ex-novios de Marisol y de Elena _____.

5. Una amiga de Elena _____.

6. Elena y su familia _____.

7. Los amigos de Pablo _____.

8. Las amigas de Elena _____.

9. Elena _____.

10. Pablo _____.

11. Los hermanos [siblings] de Elena (Erica y Felipe) y Elena_____.

12. La hermana [sister] de Elena y Elena _____.

13. Marisol _____.

14. Marisol y su familia _____.

e. Luisa está hablando con su esposo Esteban sobre los nuevos vecinos. / Luisa is talking with her husband Esteban about the new neighbors.

Completa las frases usando la forma correcta de los adjetivos y el verbo ser si es necesario. / Complete the sentences

using the correct form of the adjectives and the verb ser if it's necessary.

activo(a)   fantástico(a)   alto(a)   guapo(a)

simpático(a)   inteligente   excelente   responsable
        simpático (a)

Luisa: Alejandra es una buena persona. 1) _____ una mujer muy

2) _____. Esteban: Carlos y Pablo

3) _____ 4) _____ también [also].

Luisa: Carlos, Alejandra, Pablo y Marisol 5) _____ la familia González Fallas.

Esteban: Pablo juega tres deportes [plays three sports]. Él 6) _____ un chico 7) _____.

Luisa: Y Pablo está en la escuela secundaria [is in high school]. Sus notas [His grades] 8) _____.

9) _____. Él 10) _____ 11) _____.

Esteban: Elena y Marisol también tienen [have] notas 12) _____. Ellas 13) _____ muy

14) _____.

Respuestas correctas / Correct Answers

a. 1. informal   6. formal

2. informal*   7. formal

3. formal   8. informal

4. informal   9. formal

5. formal   10. formal

b. 1. es   6. soy

2. es   7. somos

3. es   8. es

4. son   9. son

5. soy

c. 1. llamo   8. es

2. gusto   9. Muy

3. Me llamo / Soy / Mi nombre es   10. presento a

4. presento   11. es

5. es   12. Mucho

6. es   13. son

7. Mucho gusto. / Encantado. / Es un placer.

d. 1. nosotros   8. ellas

2. ellas   9. yo

3. él   10. él

4. ellos   11. nosotros

5. ella   12. nosotras

6. nosotros   13. usted / tú

7. ellos   14. ustedes / vosotros

e. 1. Es   8. son

2. simpática / fantástica**   9. fantásticas

3. son   10. es

4. simpáticos / fantásticos   11. inteligente

5. son	12. fantásticas
6. es	13. son
7. activo	14. inteligentes

* As is the case with all of these examples, the way you address these people depends on the closeness of your relationship with them. It's also possible that you might address your uncle in a formal way.

** The word fantástica already conveys the idea of something extremely good, so it would be odd to say muy fantástica because it would be redundant. Simpática is the better answer.

Regular -ar Verbs in the Present

Vocabulario nuevo / New Vocabulary

cubano – Cuban	**salvadoreño** – Salvadoran
venezolano – Venezuelan	**paraguayo** – Paraguayan
dominicano – Dominican	**hondureño** – Honduran
colombiano – Colombian	**argentino** – Argentine
puertorriqueño – Puerto	**nicaragüense** – Nicaraguan
Rican ecuatoriano – Ecuadorian	**uruguayo** – Uruguayan
norteamericano – (North)	**costarricense** – Costa Rican
American **peruano** – Peruvian	**español** – Spaniard
mexicano – Mexican	**panameño** – Panamanian
boliviano – Bolivian	**ecuatoguineano** – Equatorial
guatemalteco – Guatemalan	Guinean
chileno – Chilean	
el café – coffee	**el trabajador** – worker
hablar – to speak, to talk	**comprar** – to buy
trabajar – to work	**cocinar** – to cook
bailar – to dance	**preparar** – to prepare
llegar – to arrive	**indicar** – to indicate
tomar – to take, to drink	**escuchar** – to hear
estudiar – to study	**ordenar** – to order
ayudar – to help	**viajar** – to travel
cantar – to sing	**dedicar** – to dedicate

fuerte – strong	**tímido** – timid
contento – happy	**malo** – bad
egoísta – selfish	**terrible** – terrible
famoso – famous	**mucho** – a lot
trabajador – hard-working	**fenomenal** – phenomenal
formal – formal	**muchos** – many
hablador – talkative	**paciente** – patient
informal – informal	**poco** – little
ideal – ideal	**impaciente** – impatient
bueno – good	**pocos** – few

Repaso general / General Review

Conjugating Verbs in Spanish

As you learned in an earlier lesson, the infinitive form of a verb is the form that appears in the dictionary and is a nonconjugated verb form. All Spanish verbs have infinitive forms ending either in **-ar, -er, or -ir,** so the three kinds of verbs in Spanish are **-ar** verbs, -er verbs, and **-ir** verbs.

The infinitive form of the verb has two parts: the stem of the word (which is everything before the ending) and the ending itself (which is either **-ar, -er, or -ir**). For example, the stem of viajar ("to travel") is **viaj-,** and the verb's ending is **-ar.** Once you've identified the stem of a verb, you conjugate the verb by adding the appropriate ending to the stem for the given subject.

Conjugating Regular -ar Verbs in the Present

The present tense endings for regular **-ar** verbs are **-o, -as, -a, -amos, -áis, and -an.** The following is an example of a regular -ar verb conjugated in the present tense.

ayudar [to help]

yo ayu**do**	nosotros, nosotras	ayud**amos**
tú ayud**as**	vosotros, vosotras	ayud**áis**
él, ella, usted ayud**a**	ellos, ellas, ustedes	ayud**an**

The verb form ayudamos, for example, can mean "We help," "We do help," "We are helping," or even—in certain contexts— "We are going to help."

When to Use Subject Pronouns before Verbs

Because the ending of a verb indicates the verb's subject, most often Spanish speakers do not include a subject pronoun before the verb. There are, however, two common cases in which subject pronouns are used. They are often used before verbs in the third-person singular and plural because there can be many possible subjects for these verb forms. Trabaja mucho, for example, could mean "You work a lot" (with the subject being usted), or it could be "He works a lot," or "She works a lot." To clarify, then, it's common to include a subject with a third-person form of the verb and say, for example, **Usted estudia mucho**.

Another time to use a subject pronoun is to emphasize the subject. If, for example, people around you are saying that they don't sing much, and you actually do, it would be appropriate to say **Yo canto mucho,** emphasizing "I do sing a lot."

More Agreement of Adjectives with Nouns

Adjectives ending in -dor in the masculine singular have four forms, as can be seen with the adjective meaning "talkative": **hablador,**

habladora, habladores, habladoras. Any adjective of nationality that ends in a consonant also has four forms, as seen in the adjective meaning "French": **francés, francesa, franceses, francesas**. Except for adjectives ending in -o, -dor, and ones ending in consonants that express nationality, almost all other adjectives in Spanish have two forms (e.g., **fenomenal, fenomenales; terrible, terribles**).

Placement of Adjectives

Adjectives in Spanish almost always follow the noun modified (e.g., **las doctoras ideales**). To modify a noun with two adjectives, put the adjectives after the noun and put y ("and") between them (e.g., **el pianista famoso y egoísta**). **Bueno** and malo can go before or after the modified noun. Before masculine nouns, both of these adjectives drop the **-o** (e.g., **el buen hombre; el mal día**). Adjectives of quantity precede the modified noun (e.g., **muchos estudiantes; poca agua**).

Pronunciation of Consonants

The double-**r** sound requires that you roll your **r**, creating a sound that does not exist in English. The sound is required when a word has the letter combination **rr**, when a word starts with **r**, and after the letters **l, n,** and **s** (e.g., **carro, Raúl, alrededor, Enrique, Israel**). You make the sound corresponding with **rr** by having your tongue vibrate up against the center of the roof of your mouth.

At the start of a word or after the letters **n** and **l**, you pronounce **d** as you would in English. After a vowel, the sound of the **d** should be like the th sound of the English word "this." When saying the name David, for example, you should pronounce the first **d** similar to the **d** sound made in English and the second **d** similar to the th of "this."

There are variations by country, but in many places, both y and ll are pronounced similar to the way y is pronounced in English.

Actividades / Activities

a. Cecilia Ruiz Ramírez es una secretaria ejecutiva en un banco muy importante de su ciudad. Ella está explicando lo que hace generalmente durante la semana. / Cecilia Ruiz Ramírez is an executive secretary at a major bank in her city. She is explaining what she usually does during the week.

Completa las frases siguientes con la conjugación del verbo en presente. / Complete the following sentences with the present tense conjugation of the verb.

Todos los días [Every day], yo 1. _____ (tomar) café con mi esposo [my husband] Luis. Mi esposo y yo 2. _____ (llegar) al trabajo [at work] a las 8:00 de la mañana. Mis colegas [my colleagues] 3. _____ (llegar) a las 8:50. Nosotros 4. _____ (tomar) café a las 10:50. En mi trabajo, (yo) 5. _____ (escuchar) a muchas personas que [that] 6.

_____ (hablar) en las reuniones [meetings]. Yo a veces [at times] 7. _____ (hablar) también [also], pero generalmente [generally] yo 8. _____ (tomar) las notas [notes] importantes de las reuniones. Mi asistente [My assistant] también 9. _____ (tomar) notas en las reuniones. Todos los días, mi asistente y yo 10. _____ (llamar) a muchas personas. También, yo 11. _____ (viajar) a dos simposios [symposiums] cada año [each year]. En casa, mi esposo y yo 12. _____ (preparar) la cena [dinner] juntos [together]. Alberto, mi hijo [son], no 13. _____ (llegar) a cenar [to have dinner] con [with] nosotros porque [because] él 14. _____ (trabajar) muy tarde [late]. Diego, mi otro [other] hijo y sus [his] amigos a veces 15. _____ (llegar) a cenar con nosotros. Ellos 16. _____ (cocinar) el postre [dessert].

b. De la historia anterior, escribe la forma negativa de los siguientes verbos. / From the previous story, write the negative form of the following verbs.

1. Mis colegas y yo _____ (tomar) café a las 11:50 de la mañana.

2. Ellos _____ (llegar) a las 7:50 de la mañana.

3. Yo _____ (hablar) nunca [never] en las reuniones.

4. Diego, mi hijo y su profesora _____ (llegar) a comer con nosotros.

c. Responde a las preguntas de forma afirmativa. / Answer the questions affirmatively.

1. ¿Bailas mucho? _____

2. ¿Clara y Roberto bailan tango? _____.

3. ¿Estudias en la universidad? _____.

4. ¿Tú y tu [your] familia preparan la cena juntos? _____.

5. ¿Tomas agua todos los días? _____.

6. ¿Isabel compra la comida en el supermercado [supermarket]? _____.

7. ¿Andrea Bocelli a veces canta en español? _____.

8. ¿Cocinas pizza con amigos? _____.

9. ¿Las chicas miran el fútbol [soccer]? _____.

10. ¿Escuchan ustedes música en el carro [car]? _____.

d. Cecilia Ruiz Ramírez está en un simposio esta semana. Ella está impresionada por la organización del simposio. / Cecilia Ruiz Ramírez is at a symposium this week. She is impressed by the organization of the symposium.

Escoge el adjetivo de cantidad correcto. / Choose the correct adjective of quantity.

1. En la mesa hay _____ (mucho, mucha, muchos, muchas) comida [food].

2. En la recepción [reception desk] hay _____ (mucho, mucha, muchos, muchas) programas [programs] del simposio.

3. En el salón [meeting room] norte hay _____ (poco, poca, pocos, pocas) café.

4. En el salón oeste hay _____ (poco, poca, pocos, pocas) personas.

5. En el salón sur hay _____ (mucho, mucha, muchos, muchas) personas.

6. En la recepción hay _____ (mucho, muchas, muchos, muchas) bebidas [drinks] pero

7. _____ (poco, poca, pocos, pocas) servilletas [napkins].

e. Luis Cortés Navarro es el dueño de una agencia de viajes. El conoce a muchas personas de distintas nacionalidades. Él está mirando un álbum de fotos y está recordando las nacionalidades de sus amigos y amigas. / Luis Cortés Navarro is the owner of a travel agency. He knows many people of different nationalities. He is looking at a photo album and is remembering his friends' nationalities.

Escoge el adjetivo correcto. / Choose the correct adjective.

1. Gerardo Martínez es muy _____ (simpático, simpática, simpáticos, simpáticas). Él es de la ciudad [city] de Guadalajara, México. Él es _____ (mexicano, mexicana, mexicanos, mexicanas).

2. Hagen Hoffmeiter y su esposa [wife] Brigitte son de Núremberg. Ellos son _____ (activo, activa, activos, activas) y son _____ (alemán, alemana, alemanes, alemanas).

3. El Rey [King] Felipe VI es de Madrid y es muy _____ (alto, alta, altos, altas). Su esposa Letizia Ortiz es de Oviedo, Asturias. Ellos son _____ (español, española, españoles, españolas).

4. Pierre Dubois es de Dijon y su familia es de Toulouse. Él es _____ (francés, francesa, franceses, francesa). Él es _____ (estudiante, estudiantes) de medicina [medicine].

5. Juan Manuel Ríos es de Buenos Aires. Él y su hermano son _____ (profesor, profesora, profesores, profesoras). Ellos son _____ (argentino, argentina, argentinos, argentinas).

6. La familia Flores Quispe es de Lima. Ellos son
_____ (peruano, peruana, peruanos, peruanas).

7. Graciela Mercedes Ramírez Villalba es _____
(dentista, dentistas). Ella trabaja en Capiatá. Ella es
_____ (paraguayo, paraguaya, paraguayos,
paraguayas).

Respuestas correctas / Correct Answers

a. 1. tomo   9. toma

2. llegamos   10. llamamos

3. llegan   11. viajo

4. tomamos   12. preparamos

5. escucho   13. llega

6. hablan   14. trabaja

7. hablo   15. llegan

8. tomo   16. cocinan

b. 1. no tomamos   3. no hablo

2. no llegan   4. no llegan

c. 1. Sí, bailo mucho.   7. Sí, Andrea Bocelli a veces canta en español.

2. Sí, Clara y Roberto bailan tango.   8. Sí, cocino pizza con amigos. / Sí, mis amigos y yo cocinamos pizza.

3. Sí, estudio en la universidad.

4. Sí, preparamos la cena juntos.   9. Sí, las chicas miran el fútbol.

5. Sí, tomo agua todos los días.   10. Sí, escuchamos música en el carro.

d. 1. mucha   5. muchas

2. muchos   6. muchas

3. poco   7. pocas

4. pocas

e. 1. simpático / mexicano   5. profesores / argentinos

2. activos / alemanes   6. peruanos

3. alto / españoles   7. dentista / paraguaya

4. francés / estudiante

Indefinite Articles and Numbers to 100

Vocabulario nuevo / New Vocabulary

un – a, an [masculine, singlar]	**una** – a, an [feminine, singular]
unos – some [masculine]	**unas** – some [feminine]
el estudiante – male student	**el zapato** – shoe
el béisbol – baseball	**el kilo** – kilo
la estudiante – female student	**el deporte** – sport
el examen – exam	**la cerveza** – beer
el águila – eagle [feminine]	
el kilómetro – kilometer	
católico – Catholic	**caminar** – to walk
extra – extra	**llevar** – to wear, to carry
enseñar – to teach	**buscar** – to look for
mirar – to look at	**necesitar** – to need
¿cuánto? – how much?	**¿cuántos?, ¿cuántas?** – how many?
para – for	**por favor** – please
cero – zero	**cinco** – five
uno – one	**seis** – six
dos – two	**siete** – seven

tres – three **cuatro** – four **ocho** – eight	**nueve** – nine **diez** – ten
once – eleven **doce** – twelve **trece** – thirteen **catorce** – fourteen **quince** – fifteen	**dieciséis** – sixteen **diecisiete** – seventeen **dieciocho** – eighteen **diecinueve** – nineteen **veinte** – twenty
treinta – thirty **cuarenta** – forty **cincuenta** – fifty **sesenta** – sixty	**setenta** – seventy **ochenta** – eighty **noventa** – ninety **cien** – one hundred

Repaso general / General Review

Improving Your Ability to Communicate in Spanish

Being proficient in Spanish really means performing it as needed. And proper performance of Spanish—when speaking or writing—happens only as the result of sufficient practice. That's why the most effective way to improve your ability to communicate in Spanish is to practice it as much as possible, whether by engaging with the audio glossary, speaking activities, and workbook or by interacting with other Spanish speakers. Also, try to use Spanish even when you're not studying the language by, for example, counting in Spanish in your daily life. The more contact you have with Spanish—the more you speak it, read it, write it, or hear it—the quicker and more fully you will acquire the language.

Indefinite Articles

While "a" and "an" (in the singular) and "some" (in the plural) are the indefinite articles in English, in Spanish there are four forms of the indefinite article: **un** (masculine singular), **una** (feminine singular), **unos** (masculine plural), unas (feminine plural). Examples of indefinite articles used with nouns include **un zapato** [a shoe], una **cerveza** [a beer], **unos kilómetros** [some kilometers], and **unas águilas** [some eagles].

In general, the indefinite article in Spanish is used much as it is in English. For example, "Carlos is taking an exam" is **Carlos toma un examen**. Unlike English, indefinite articles are typically not used when talking about one's profession, religion, or nationality (e.g., "María is a doctor" is **María es doctora**; "Pedro is a Catholic" **is Pedro es católico**; "Teresa is a Spaniard" is **Teresa es española**). When, however, the profession, religion, or nationality is modified by an adjective, then an indefinite article is used (e.g., **María es una doctora excelente; Pedro es un buen católico; Teresa es una española famosa**).

Feminine nouns beginning with the sound a in a stressed syllable use **un** rather than **una** as their indefinite article. **Un** águila [an eagle], for example, is indeed a feminine noun, but it uses un rather than **una** as its indefinite article. [Note: If una were used as the definite article for águila, then the two a sounds would run together when pronounced and sound like unaaáguila; using **un** instead of **una** avoids this problem.] Feminine nouns beginning with the sound a in a syllable that is not stressed keep the usual definite article of una (e.g., **una actitud** [an attitude]).

Numbers 1 to 100

Once you learn the numbers one to ten, you can use those numbers to help you learn ten to twenty and then the multiples of ten from ten to one hundred. Notice the similarities and differences in the following numbers.

uno	once	diez
dos	doce	veinte
tres	trece	treinta
cuatro	catorce	cuarenta
cinco	quince	cincuenta
seis	dieciséis	sesenta
siete	diecisiete	setenta
ocho	dieciocho	ochenta
nueve	diecinueve	noventa
diez	veinte	cien

Usually, a number doesn't change its form when modifying a noun. For example, **siete** stays the same in **Hay siete** chicos and **Hay siete chicas**. Numbers that do change are those ending in **-un** or **-una**. For example, "twenty-one men" uses the masculine form **veintiún hombres,** while "forty-one women" uses the feminine form **cuarenta y una mujeres.**

Pronunciation

The Spanish letters **b** and **v** are associated with the same sound: the sound made when a **b** is pronounced in English. Like the sound associated with the letter t, the sounds associated with the letters **p, b,**

v, and **k** in Spanish are not aspirated, meaning that you produce no puff of air when you pronounce words with these letters in them. When you say, for example, Bolivia or El taco es para Teresa, your mouth should produce no puffs of air. You can test this by putting your hand in front of your mouth when speaking; your hand should not feel any puffs of air when you pronounce the sounds associated with **t, p, b, v**, and **k.**

The letters k and w are hardly used in Spanish because they only appear in words that come from other languages (e.g., **el kilo, el whisky**). The sound associated with the letter w in Spanish is the same as it is in English.

The sounds made when pronouncing the letters c and g are as follows: The **k** sound is made when **c** appears before **a, o,** or **u** (e.g., **la casa, el taco, Cuba**); in Latin America, the s sound is made when **c** appears before e or i, while in Spain, the sound made is th, as in the English word "this." So, Latin Americans would pronounce **cero** and **cinco** by saying these words with an s sound, while someone from Madrid would say these words with a **th** sound. The sound associated with **z** is always the same as the sound associated with ce and **ci:** Latin Americans would say **zapato** [shoe] by pronouncing an s sound, while someone from Madrid would pronounce the word with a th sound.

The letter **g** is like **c** because the way it's pronounced depends on the letter that follows it: The hard **g** sound is made when g is followed by **a, o,** or **u** (e.g., la galleta [cookie], Gonzalo, Gustavo); the Spanish j sound is made when the letter following g is e or i (e.g., Argentina, **el gigante** [giant]).

The letter **x** in Spanish is usually associated with the same sound produced by the **x** in English (e.g., **el taxi**). With certain Mexican place names, the **x** is pronounced with the sound made by jota (e.g., **México**); at other times, the **x** is pronounced as an s, as in **el xilófono** [xylophone]. The letter **ñ** is associated with the sound made in the English word "onion" (e.g., España).

Actividades / Activities

a. Marisol asiste ahora a una nueva escuela secundaria: la escuela Miguel de Cervantes. Marisol habla con su madre Alejandra sobre las cosas que se encuentran en su aula de biología. / Marisol is now attending a new high school: Miguel de Cervantes High School. Marisol talks to her mother Alejandra about the things that can be found in her biology classroom.

Agrega el artículo indefinido apropiado. / Add the correct indefinite article.

En el aula [classroom] hay:

1. _____ lápices

2. _____ mesa

3. _____ exámenes

9. _____ esqueleto [skeleton]

10. _____ sillas

11. _____ televisor

4. _____ reloj   12. _____ mapas

5. _____ libros   13. _____ teléfono

6. _____ computadoras [computers]   14. _____ maestra
[teacher]

7. _____ cuadernos   15. _____ chicos

8. _____ diccionarios [dictionaries]   16. _____ estudiantes altas

b. El padre de Marisol, Carlos González, quiere aprender a hacer algo nuevo en su tiempo libre. / Marisol's father, Carlos González, wants to learn how to do something new in his free time.

Completa las frases con el artículo indefinido correcto. / Complete the sentences with the correct indefinite article.

Carlos quiere aprender a hacer algo nuevo. Él mira 1. _____ sitios web [websites] interesantes. 2. _____ amigo le recomendó [recommended to him] tomar 3. _____ curso en casa. Ahora él busca 4. _____ curso de fotografía [photography] de The Great Courses. Él necesita 5. _____ cámara [camera], 6. _____ ideas [ideas] y 7. _____ buena actitud.

c. La familia González Fallas está conociendo a los vecinos de Villa Celeste. Ellos hablan sobre las profesiones que todos tienen. / The

González Fallas family is getting to know their neighbors in Villa Celeste. They talk about the professions that everyone has.

Completa las frases con el artículo indefinido correcto. Si la frase no necesita un artículo, escribe "X". / Complete the sentences with the correct indefinite article. If the sentence does not need an article, write an "X."

Luis Cortés es 1. _____ dueño [owner] de una agencia de viajes. Su [His] esposa [wife] Cecilia es 2. _____ secretaria ejecutiva. Cecilia es 3. _____ secretaria excelente. Su hijo [son] Alberto es 4. _____ dentista fantástico. Su hijo Diego es 5. _____ estudiante. Su hijo Javier es 6. _____ ingeniero [engineer] muy responsable. El otro [other] vecino, Esteban Quirós, no solo es 7. _____ doctor, él es 8. _____ doctor muy famoso en el hospital. Luisa, la esposa de Esteban, es 9. _____ nutricionista [nutritionist]. Ella es 10. _____ nutricionista muy trabajadora.

d. Escribe los números correctos. / Write the correct numbers.

1. ¿Cuántos estados [states] hay en los Estados Unidos?

_____.

2. ¿Cuántos días hay en enero [January]?

_____.

3. ¿Cuántos días hay en un febrero [February] normal?

_____.

4. ¿Cuántas dedos [fingers] hay en dos manos?

_____.

5. ¿Cuántas semanas [weeks] hay en un año [year]?

_____.

6. En la canción [song] "The Twelve Days of Christmas" [Los doce días de la Navidad], ¿cuántas mujeres bailan? _____.

7. ¿En cuántas naciones de América Central se habla [is spoken] español como lengua oficial? _____.

Lectura cultural / Cultural Reading

Lee el texto siguiente sobre la comida latinoamericana y contesta las preguntas de forma cierto ("C") o falso ("F"). / Read the following text about Latin American food and answer the questions as either true ("C") or false ("F").

La comida latinoamericana es más que burritos, quesadillas y tacos. Aunque en los Estados Unidos una de las comidas más conocida es la comida mexicana, esta también está compuesta de una gran variedad de ingredientes, colores y sabores. En la comida latinoamericana hay una mezcla de cultura con influencia indígena y europea, por ejemplo, de España, Italia, e incluso de África.

Es importante notar que la comida varía según la región geográfica y el país. Estas variaciones gastronómicas dependen de los productos de cada región, de la cercanía con el mar, de la geografía particular de cada zona y de las tradiciones y orígenes culturales de cada pueblo. Por ejemplo, en el norte de México los tamales se envuelven con las hojas de maíz y en el sur con las hojas del plátano. Pero en general, en todo México se utilizan distintos tipos de chiles para sazonar las comidas y por eso es común que la comida mexicana sea muy picante. Los elementos básicos en el país son las tortillas, el arroz, los frijoles, el ajo y los chiles picantes.

En Centroamérica, las comidas son similares a México, pero cada país tiene sus propios platos típicos. También, en las costas se utilizan muchos mariscos que pueden prepararse en estofados, a la parrilla, crudos, o encurtidos como el ceviche. Aunque el ceviche se come en Centroamérica y América del Sur, es especialmente famoso el de Perú. El ceviche básico consiste en pescado crudo marinado en cítricos como el limón. Se le agregan condimentos como cebolla, chile, pimienta y sal.

En el caso de la carne de res, los argentinos y uruguayos son los más conocidos en consumo y preparación de carnes, seguidos de los colombianos, venezolanos y brasileños. El plátano es muy común en platos de comida colombiana y centroamericana. Los patacones (plátanos verdes fritos) de Colombia son famosos e indispensables en lacomida colombiana. Son tradicionales también en los platos venezolanos y puertorriqueños, pero estos últimos les llaman tostones.

1. La comida latinoamericana consiste solo en burritos, tacos y quesadillas. _____

2. La comida latinoamericana tiene una influencia indígena y europea. _____

3. Los tamales en el norte y el sur de México son diferentes. _____

4. Dos elementos básicos de la comida de México son los chiles picantes y los tostones. _____

5. Los argentinos y uruguayos son famosos por la preparación de la carne de res. _____

Respuestas correctas / Correct Answers

a. 1. unos	9. un
2. una	10. unas
3. unos	11. un
4. un	12. unos
5. unos	13. un
6. unas	14. una
7. unos	15. unos
8. unos	16 unas

b. 1. unos   5. una

2. Un   6. unas

3. un   7. una

4. un

c. 1. X   6. un

2. X   7. X

3. una   8. un

4. un   9. X

5. X   10. una

d. 1. cincuenta   5. cincuenta y dos

2. treinta y uno   6. nueve

3. veintiocho   7. seis

4. diez

Lectura cultural

1. F   2. C   3. C   4. F   5. C

Latin American food is more than burritos, quesadillas, and tacos. Even though in the United States Mexican food is one of the most well-known kinds, Mexican food is also composed of a great variety of ingredients, colors, and flavors. In Latin American food, there is a mixture of culture with indigenous and European influence from, for example, Spain, Italy, and even Africa.

It's important to note that food varies according to geographical region and country. These gastronomic variations depend on the products of each region, proximity to the sea, the particular geography of each zone, and the traditions and cultural origins of each nation. For example, in the north of Mexico tamales are wrapped in corn husks and in the south in banana leaves. But in general, in all of Mexico, different types of chili peppers are used to season food, and for that reason it's common for Mexican food to be spicy. The basic elements in the country are tortillas, rice, beans, garlic, and hot chilis.

In Central America, the food is similar to Mexican food, but each country has its own typical dishes. Also, on the coasts many shellfish are used that can be prepared in stews, on the grill, raw, or pickled as in ceviche. Although ceviche is eaten in Central America and South America, it is especially famous in Peru. Basic ceviche consists of raw fish marinated in citrus fruit like lemon. Condiments like onion, chili peppers, pepper, and salt are added to it.

The Argentines and the Uruguayans are the most known for consuming and cooking beef, followed by the Colombians,

Venezuelans, and Brazilians. Bananas are very common in dishes of Colombian and Central American food. **Patacones** (fried green bananas) from Colombia are famous and indispensable in Colombian food. They are also traditional in Venezuelan and Puerto Rican dishes, but people there call them **tostones.**

The Verb Estar and Numbers over 100

Vocabulario nuevo / New Vocabulary

caliente – hot	**tranquilo** – calm
aburrido – bored	**desordenado** – disorganized, messy
frío – cold	
cansado – tired	**triste** – sad
nervioso – nervous	**roto** – broken
enfermo – sick	**alegre** – happy
preocupado – worried	**abierto** – open
ocupado – busy	**enojado** – angry
frustrado – frustrated	**cerrado** – closed
preparado – prepared	**feliz** – happy
confundido – confused	**ordenado** – organized, tidy
estar – to be **¡Repitan!** – Repeat! [formal command]	**¡Empecemos!** – Let's get started!
el parque – park **iglesia** – church **el hospital** – hospital **el aeropuerto** – airport **la biblioteca** – library	**la tienda** – store **el carro** – car **la oficina** – office **el dólar** – dollar **el mercado** – market
antes de Cristo – B.C.	**después de Cristo** – A.D.

cien – one hundred	**setecientos** – seven hundred
doscientos – two hundred	**ochocientos** – eight hundred
trescientos – three hundred	**ochocientos** – eight hundred
cuatrocientos – four hundred	**ochocientos** – eight hundred
quinientos – five hundred	**millón** – million
seiscientos – six hundred	

Repaso general / General Review

Approach to Learning New Verbs

The three questions you should ask when learning any new verb are as follows.

1. What does it mean?

2. How do you use it?

3. How do you conjugate it?

The Verb estar

Using these three questions with our new verb produces the following answers.

1. The verb **estar** means "to be."

2. **Estar** has three main uses, and the two you'll examine now are a) **estar** used to express the state or condition of someone or something

(e.g., "I'm well" is **Estoy bien;** "The coffee is hot" **is El café está caliente**) and b) **estar** used to express location (e.g., **¿Estás en la tienda?** is "Are you in the store?," except when talking about origin, when ser is used: **Soy de Sevilla** is "I am from Sevilla").

3. The conjugation of **estar** is as follows.

estar [to be]

yo	estoy	nosotros, nosotras	estamos
tú	estás	vosotros, vosotras	estáis
él, ella, usted	está	ellos, ellas, ustedes	están

The yo form of estar has the same -oy ending as the yo form of ser. The other five endings for estar are almost the same as the regular -ar endings (except that the endings for estar have accents in the tú, usted, and ustedes forms).

Communicating beyond Words

When speaking, make sure to use tone of voice, facial expressions, and gestures to communicate in addition to the words you're saying. Thinking about the words you want to say requires significant mental energy for a beginning language learner, but focusing only on the words you're saying can produce a robotic speech, devoid of emotion. So, when speaking, do your best to remember to make use of your tone of voice, face, and body as tools to help you convey your message.

Numbers over 100

Use the numbers one to ten to help you learn the multiples of one hundred from one hundred to one thousand. Notice the similarities and differences in the following numbers.

uno	once
dos	doscientos
tres	trescientos
cuatro	cuatrocientos
cinco	quinientos
seis	seiscientos
siete	setecientos
ocho	ochocientos
nueve	novecientos
diez	mil

"One hundred cars" is **cien carros** and "one thousand churches" is **mil iglesias,** but "one million dollars" is **un millón de dólares.** Examples of years in Spanish are the following: 1578 is **mil quinientos setenta y ocho** and 2019 is **dos mil diecienueve.**

In much of the Spanish-speaking world, the use of periods and commas with numbers is the opposite of what it is in the United States.

So, what in the United States would be written as 23,400.50 would be written as 23.400,50.

Differences in Accents

In all regions where Spanish is spoken, **ce** and **ci** are always pronounced the same as **z**. In Latin America, **z** makes the s sound, as seen in the pronunciation of the words **cero, cinco,** and **zapato**, which in Latin America are pronounced as "**sero**," "**sinco**," and "**sapato**." This is called the seseo variety of Spanish. In northern and central Spain, where s is pronounced as an s and **z** is pronounced as th, these words are pronounced "**thero**," "**thinco**," and "**thapato**." This accent, which shows a distinction between the pronunciation of s and th sounds, is called the distinción variety of Spanish, and it characterizes the Spanish spoken in northern and central Spain. Finally, there are just a few areas in very southern Spain where the letters **s** and **z** are pronounced the same, but the sound made for both letters sounds like th. This rare variety of Spanish is called the **ceceo** variety.

In 1492, when Spaniards first went to the Americas, the Spanish spoken in Spain was the **seseo** variety. During the 16th century, distinción developed in Spain, but primarily in the northern and central parts of the country. So, by the late 1500s, a Spaniard living in Madrid or in a more northern city would be pronouncing words in a way that distinguished between the **z** of **zapato** and the s of casa. Many of the Spaniards that emigrated from the Iberian Peninsula came from

Andalusia in southern Spain or from the Canary Islands, areas that never developed the distinción that characterized more northern speech. That's why speakers in Sevilla even today pronounce the **z** like Latin Americans instead of like people from Madrid. Because speakers in southern areas spoke the **seseo** variety of Spanish and because so many of them went to the Americas, the **seseo** variety of Spanish became the standard in Latin America.

Actividades / Activities

a. Juan Manuel Ríos, el amigo argentino de Luis Cortés, está de visita en Villa Celeste. Luis Cortés les está presentando a Juan Manuel a sus vecinos. / Juan Manuel Ríos, the Argentine friend of Luis Cortés, is visiting Villa Celeste. Luis Cortés is introducing Juan Manuel to his neighbors.

Completa el diálogo siguiente con las palabras y las conjugaciones apropiadas del verbo estar. / Complete the following dialogue with the appropriate words and verb conjugations of estar.

cansado   igualmente   es un placer   argentino   días
feliz (2)   estar (5)

Alejandra: Buenos 1. _____, Luis.

Luis: Hola, Alejandra. ¿Cómo 2. _____? Te presento a Juan Manuel. Él es mi amigo de Argentina.

Alejandra: ¡Hola, Juan Manuel! 3. _____.

Juan Manuel: 4. ¡_____!

Luisa: ¿Eres 5. _____? ¡Qué interesante!

Juan Manuel: Sí, mi familia y yo vivimos en Buenos Aires.

Luisa: ¿Y cómo estás?

Juan Manuel: Bueno [Well], 6. _____ muy 7. _____. Mi vuelo [flight] tardó [took] muchas horas [hours]. Pero 8. _____ 9._____ porque [because] Luis es mi buen amigo y ahora [now] estoy con [with] él y su familia.

Luis: Y Cecilia y yo 10._____ muy 11. _____ porque Juan Manuel 12. _____ de visita.

b. De acuerdo a las siguientes situaciones, ¿cuál sería la emoción o la condición esperada para estas personas? / According to the following situations, what would be the expected emotion or condition for these people?

Completa las frases con la conjugación apropiada de estar y el adjetivo correspondiente a la situación. / Complete the sentences with the appropriate conjugation of estar and the adjective corresponding to the situation.

enamorado [in love]   enojado   nervioso   aburrido

frustrado   feliz   cansado

1. Luis Cortés trabaja muchas horas en su trabajo. Él siempre [always]

_____.

2. Cecilia tiene que [has to] preparar un informe financiero [financial report] en quince minutos [minutes]. Ella _____ muy

_____.

3. Juana está divorciada [divorced]. Él y su ex-esposo [ex-husband] no

_____.

4. Mariana es muy pequeña y siempre toma los juguetes [toys] de Diana cuando están en el parque. Diana _____

_____.

5. Hay un examen en la clase a las 8:00. Los estudiantes

_____ _____.

6. Erica está embarazada [pregnant]. Ella y su esposo _____ muy _____.

7. Alberto, un hombre de treinta y cinco años [years], vive en la casa de sus padres y tiene [has] pocos amigos. Él _____

_____.

8. Alberto también es egoísta y no ayuda a sus padres a limpiar [to clean] la casa. Sus padres _____ _____ con él.

9. Generalmente [Generally], ¿cómo estás en una fiesta [party]?

_____ _____.

c. Felipe tuvo una fiesta anoche y ahora está revisando su casa después de la fiesta. Toda la casa es un desastre. / Felipe had a party last night and is now looking over his house after the party. The whole house is a disaster.

Completa las frases con la conjugación de estar y el adjetivo de condición apropiados. / Complete the sentences with the appropriate conjugation of estar and the appropriate adjective of condition.

abierto   roto   ordenado   cerrado
            desordenado

Felipe está muy preocupado y nervioso porque después de la fiesta toda la casa 1. _____

2. _____. Todas las puertas [doors] 3. _____ 4. _____, y el televisor 5. _____ 6. _____. Las ventanas [windows] de la casa 7. _____ 8. _____, y hay mucho polen [pollen] en el aire. Solo el baño [bathroom] 9. _____ 10. _____.

d. Escribe en qué lugares se pueden localizar las siguientes personas o cosas. / Write in which places the following people or things can be found.

iglesia   oficina   biblioteca supermercado

universidad   hospital   parque [supermarket]

1. Las doctoras trabajan en los _____.

2. Los libros y las revistas [magazines] están en la

_____.

3. Una secretaria ejecutiva [executive secretary] generalmente trabaja

en una _____.

4. Siempre compro mucha agua en el _____.

5. Los profesores enseñan cursos en las

_____.

6. Los domingos [On Sundays] hay muchas personas en las

_____.

7. Los chicos corren en los _____.

e. Escribe los siguientes años en español. / Write the following years in Spanish.

1. 1886 _____

2. 2019 _____

3. 1605 _____

4. 319 A.D. _____

5. 711 B.C. _____

6. 1942 _____

7. 2034 _____

Respuestas correctas / Correct Answers

a. 1. días   7. cansado

2. estás   8. estoy

3. Es un placer   9. feliz

4. Igualmente   10. estamos

5. argentino   11. felices

6. Estoy   12. está

b. 1. está cansado   6. están muy felices

2. está muy nerviosa   7. está aburrido / está frustrado

3. están enamorados frustrados   8. están enojados / están

4. está frustrada / está enojada   9. Estoy feliz

5. están nerviosos

c. 1. está   6. roto

2. desordenada   7. están

3. están   8. abiertas

4. abiertas / cerradas   9. está

5. está   10. ordenado

d. 1. hospitales   5. universidades

2. biblioteca   6. iglesias

3. oficina   7. parques

4. supermercado

e. 1. mil ochocientos ochenta y seis   5. setecientos once antes
de Cristo

2. dos mil diecienueve   6. mil novecientos
cuarenta y dos

3. mil seiscientos cinco   7. dos mil treinta y cuatro

4. trescientos diecinueve después de Cristo

Regular -er and -ir Verbs in the Present

Vocabulario nuevo / New Vocabulary

comer – to eat	**vivir** – to live
leer – to read	**abrir** – to open
beber – to drink	ecibir – to receive
creer – to believe, to think	**descubrir** – to discover
aprender – to learn	**subir** – to go up
correr – to run	**escribir** – to write
vender – to sell	**decidir** – to decide
deber – should	**asistir a** – to attend
asistir a – to attend	
mi / mis – my	**nuestro(s) / nuestra(s)** – our
tu / tus – your [informal, singular]	**vuestro(s) / vuestra(s)** – your [informal, plural]
su / sus – his, her, their, your [formal, singular, and plural]	
¿no? – Isn't that so?	**¿cierto?** – right?
¿verdad? – right?	
los parientes – relatives	**el abuelo** – grandfather
los padres – parents	**la abuela** – grandmother
la madre – mother	**el tío** – uncle
la mamá – mom	**la tía** – aunt
mami – mommy	**el primo** – male cousin
el padre – father	**la prima** – female cousin
el papá – dad	**el sobrino** – nephew
papi – daddy	**la sobrina** – niece

el esposo – husband **la esposa** – wife **el hijo** – son **la hija** – daughter **el hermano** – brother **la hermana** – sister	**el nieto** – grandson **la nieta** – granddaughter **el nombre** – name **el apellido** – last name **materno** – maternal **paterno** – paternal
la computadora – computer **el diccionario** – dictionary	**el trabajo** – work, job **la pluma** – pen

Repaso general / General Review

Conjugation of Regular Verbs

In a previous lesson, you learned that -ar verbs have the following endings in the present.

estudiar [to study]

estu**dio**	estud**iamos**
estud**ias**	estud**iáis**
estud**ia**	estud**ian**

In this lesson, you learned that **-er** verb endings in the present can be formed by making just one change to the above **-ar** endings: Replace any a you see in an **-ar** ending with the letter **e**. Making that one change gives us the following **-er** endings in the present.

beber [to drink]

beb**o**	bebem**os**
beb**es**	beb**éis**
beb**e**	beb**en**

Making the following two changes to **-er** endings gives us the **-ir** endings in the present: **emos à imos, éis à ís**. Those two changes give us the following **-ir** endings in the present.

dedidir [to decide]

decid**o**	decidim**os**
decid**es**	decid**ís**
decid**e**	decid**en**

When two verbs are used together, you conjugate the first and put the second in the infinitive form. This can be seen with a first verb like **deber** (should) or **necesitar** (to need). "We should run" is Debemos correr. "They need to open the book" is **Necesitan abrir el libro.** In both of these cases, the first verb (**debemos, necesitan**) is conjugated, while the second verb (**correr, abrir**) is in the infinitive form.

Possessive Adjectives

Possessive adjectives agree in number and gender with the thing possessed. They are as follows.

mi / mis [my]   nuestro / nuestra / nuestros / nuestras [our]

tu / tus [your (informal)]   vuestro / vuestra / vuestros / vuestras [your (informal)]

su / sus [his, her, your (formal, singular)]   su / sus [their, your (formal, plural)]

Asking a Yes/No Question

There are three ways to ask yes/no questions in Spanish.

1. Raise the pitch of your voice at the end of the sentence.

2. End the sentence with ¿no? [Isn't that so?], **¿verdad?** [right?], or **¿cierto?** [right?].

3. Put the verb before the subject.

Here are the ways to make the following statement into a question: **Pedro vende su casa**. [Pablo is selling his house.]

1. **¿Pedro vende su casa?** (Say it with a rising pitch at the end of the sentence.)

2. **Pedro vende su casa, ¿no?; Pedro vende su casa, ¿verdad?; Pedro vende su casa, ¿cierto?**

3. **¿Vende Pedro su casa?**

Actividades / Activities

a. Marisol está hablando por Skype con sus amigas Pilar y Carolina sobre su nueva escuela. / Marisol is talking on Skype with her friends Pilar and Carolina about her new school.

Completa el diálogo siguiente con los adjetivos posesivos apropiados. / Complete the following dialogue with the appropriate possessive adjectives.

Marisol: ¡Hola! ¿Cómo están?

Pilar: ¡Nosotras estamos muy bien! ¿Y tú?

Marisol: Estoy un poco triste porque no estoy con ustedes, pero estoy bien.

Carolina: ¿Cómo es 1. _____ nueva escuela?

Marisol: Es muy grande y muy bonita. 2. _____ clase de inglés es excelente y

3. _____ libros para la clase son muy interesantes.

Carolina: Marisol, ¿Hay muchos estudiantes en 4. _____ clase de inglés?

Marisol: En 5. _____ clase hay 35 estudiantes.

Pilar: Carolina y yo estamos en una clase de historia fenomenal y en una clase de matemáticas terrible. En

6. _____ clase de historia también hay 35 estudiantes, pero en 7. _____

clase de matemáticas solo hay 15 estudiantes.

Carolina: ¿Qué tal son los maestros [teachers] en la nueva escuela?

Marisol: 8. Todos _____ maestros son inteligentes, pero no todos son simpáticos.

b. Felipe está limpiando su casa después de una fiesta. Hay muchos objetos, pero Felipe no sabe a quiénes pertenecen. Felipe está hablando con su hermana Elena sobre los objetos encontrados. / Felipe is cleaning his house after a party. There are many objects, but Felipe doesn't know to whom they belong. Felipe is talking with his sister Elena about the found objects.

Completa las frases con los adjetivos posesivos correctos. / Complete the sentences with the correct possessive adjectives.

1. Felipe: Elena, el teléfono celular es de Rogelio, ¿cierto?

Elena: No, es _____ teléfono celular.

a) vuestros b) mi c) su

2. Felipe: Elena, el libro de Isabel Allende es de mami, ¿cierto?

Elena: No, es de _____ amiga Maribel.

a) su b) vuestras c) sus

3. Felipe: Elena, los papeles son de Mariana, ¿verdad?

Elena: No, son de _____ tía.

a) nuestros b) mis c) nuestra

4. Felipe: Elena, las iPads son de Margarita y Lourdes, ¿no?

Elena: No, son de _____ amigos David y Miguel.

a) mi b) tus c) nuestro

5. Felipe: Elena, las plumas son de Sebastián, ¿no?

Elena: No, son _____ plumas.

a) tu b) nuestros c) mis

6. Felipe: Elena, los cuadernos son de Sandra y Valentina, ¿verdad?

Elena: No, son de _____ sobrinas Diana y Mariana.

a) nuestras b) nuestra c) vuestra

c. Contesta las siguientes preguntas. Conjuga el verbo en el presente. / Answer the following questions. Conjugate the verb in the present.

1. Lees libros de ciencia ficción [science fiction], ¿no? _____.

2. Bebes mucha agua, ¿verdad? _____.

3. Tú y tu amigo vendéis carros en vuestro trabajo, ¿cierto? _____.

4. Trabajas 40 horas a la semana [hours per week], ¿verdad? _____.

5. Tú y tu familia comen pizza en casa, ¿verdad? _____.

6. Tú y tu familia viven en los Estados Unidos, ¿cierto? _____.

7. ¿Los estudiantes asisten a una buena escuela? _____.

8. ¿Deben estudiar música tus hermanos? _____.

d. Luis Cortés le está explicando a su amigo Juan Manuel Ríos el parentesco de sus amigos en el vecindario. / Luis Cortés is explaining to his friend Juan Manuel Ríos the kinship of his friends in the neighborhood.

Completa las frases con la información apropiada. Nota: Necesitas consultar la información de las familias del vecindario al inicio del cuaderno. / Complete the sentences with the appropriate information. Note: You need to consult the information about the neighborhood families at the beginning of the workbook.

1. Diana es la _____ de Luis y Cecilia.

a) hermana b) hija c) nieta

2. Javier es el _____ de Luis y Cecilia.

a) abuelo b) hijo c) sobrino

3. Mariana es la _____ de Diana.

a) nieta b) abuela c) hermana

4. Carlos es el _____ de Pablo y Marisol.

a) padre c) tío c) sobrino

5. Erica, Felipe y Elena son los _____ de Esteban y Luisa.

a) nietos b) hijos c) primos

6. Erica es la _____ de Javier.

a) prima b) hermana c) esposa

7. Carlos es el _____ de Alejandra.

a) tío b) esposo c) nieto

8. Mariana es la _____ de Diego.

a) hija b) hermana c) sobrina

9. Luis y Cecilia son los _____ de Diana.

a) tíos b) primos c) abuelos

10. Alberto y Diego son los _____ de Mariana.

a) primos b) tíos c) hijos

e. ¡Ahora es tu turno! Contesta las siguientes preguntas. / Now it's your turn! Answer the following questions.

1. ¿Quiénes son tus padres? _____.

2. ¿Quiénes son tus hermanos? _____.

3. ¿Quiénes son tus abuelos? _____.

4. El hijo de tu hija es tu _____.

5. Los padres de tu padre son tus _____.

6. Las hijas de tu hermano son tus _____.

7. La hija de tus tíos es tu _____.

8. Los hermanos de tu madre son tus _____.

f. ¿Puedes adivinar los apellidos de las siguientes personas? / Can you guess the last names of the following people?

1. Padres: Luis Cortés Navarro y Cecilia Ruiz Ramírez.

Hijo: Alberto _____.

2. Padres: Esteban Quirós Sánchez y Luisa García Vega.

Hija: Elena _____.

3. Padres: Carlos González Pérez y Alejandra Fallas Ureña.

Hijo: Pablo _____.

Respuestas correctas / Correct Answers

a. 1. tu

2. Mi / Nuestra

3. mis / nuestros

4. tu

5. mi / nuestra

6. nuestra

7. nuestra

8. mis / nuestros

b. 1. b) mi

2. a) su

3. c) nuestra

4. b) tus

5. c) mis

6. a) nuestras

c. 1. Sí, leo libros de ciencia ficción. / No, no leo libros de ciencia ficción.

2. Sí, bebo mucha agua. / No, no bebo mucha agua.

3. Sí, vendemos carros en nuestro trabajo. / No, no vendemos carros en nuestro trabajo.

4. Sí, trabajo 40 horas a la semana. / No, no trabajo 40 horas a la semana.

5. Sí, comemos pizza en casa. / No, no comemos pizza en casa.

6. Sí, vivimos en los Estados Unidos. / No, no vivimos en los Estados Unidos.

7. Sí, los estudiantes asisten a una buena escuela. / No, los estudiantes asisten a una mala escuela.

8. Sí, mis hermanos deben estudiar música. / No, mis hermanos no deben estudiar música.

d. 1. c) nieta   6. c) esposa

2. b) hijo   7. b) esposo

3. c) hermana   8. c) sobrina

4. a) padre   9. c) abuelos

5. b) hijos   10. b) tíos

e. 1. Mis padres son….   5. abuelos

2. Mis hermanos son…. / Soy hijo/hija único/única.   6. sobrinas

3. Mis abuelos son….   7. prima

4. nieto   8. tíos

f. 1. Alberto Cortés Ruiz

2. Elena Quirós García

3. Pablo González Fallas

The Verb Ir in the Present

Vocabulario nuevo / New Vocabulary

nuevo – new	**interrogativo** – interrogative
la manera – way **la palabra** – word **el vocabulario** – vocabulary **el verbo** – verb **el sustantivo** – noun	**el adjetivo** – adjective **el adverbio** – adverb **la preposición** – preposition **la tarea** – homework, chore
ir – to go **pasar** – to happen	**terminar** – to finish
¿cómo? – how? **¿qué?** – what? **¿dónde?** – where? **¿adónde?** – to where?	**¿quién?** – who? [singular] **¿quiénes?** – who? [plural] **¿por qué?** – why? **¿cuándo?** – when?
la escuela – school **el restaurante** – restaurant **la plaza** – city square, town square **el museo** – museum **el banco** – bank **la farmacia** – pharmacy **el supermercado** – supermarket **el teatro** – theater	**el cine** – movie theater **el club** – club **el café** – café **la estación de trenes** – train station **la estación de autobuses** – bus station **los servicios sanitarios** – restrooms **el baño** – bathroom
mañana – tomorrow **a** – to ahora **más**–more **posiblemente** – possibly	**porque** – because **mismo** – right now **¿Qué pasa?** – What's happening?

Repaso general / General Review

Spelling Changes for y and o

In a previous lesson, you learned that y means "and" and o means "or." In this lesson, you learned the following spelling changes: y becomes e before a word beginning with an i sound; o becomes u before a word beginning with an o sound. Examples of these changes include Roberto e Isabel [Robert and Isabel] and minuto u hora [minute or hour].

Ir in the Present

The verb ir, meaning "to go," has the following conjugation in the present.

ir [to go]

voy	**vamos**
vas	**vais**
va	**van**

The yo form of **voy** is similar to the yo form of **ser** [to be], which is **soy** [I am]. The other five endings **[-as, -a, -amos, -ais, -an]** are the same as the endings for regular **-ar** verbs, with only one difference: There is no accent over the a in the vosotros form **vais**.

The preposition a, meaning "to," is often used after **ir.** For example, **Elena va a la farmacia** means "Elena goes / is going / does go to the pharmacy." When used before the masculine definite article **el** [the], **a + el** contracts to al [to the], so "I am going to the bank" is **Voy al banco**. In a previous lesson, you learned that **de + el** contracts to del [to the] (e.g., **Es el día del examen** is "It's the day of the exam"). The only two contractions in Spanish are **al** and **del**.

Ir Used to Talk about a Future Event

The construction **ir + a + infinitivo** [infinitive] is used to talk about a future event by expressing something that is going to occur, so **Vamos a caminar al supermercado** is "We are going to walk to the supermarket," and **Voy a comer** is "I am going to eat."

Palabras interrogativas / Interrogative Words

Interrogative words are used when asking questions. These words, which all have an accent mark, include **¿cuánto?** [how much?], **¿cuántos?** [how many?], **¿cómo?** [how?], **¿qué?** [what?], ¿dónde? [where?], **¿adónde?** [to where?], **¿cuándo?** [when?], **¿quién?** [who? (singular)], **¿quiénes?** [who? (plural)], and **¿por qué?** [why?].

Uses of estar and ser

In general, **estar** is used to talk about location (e.g., **¿Dónde están los estudiantes?** is "Where are the students?"; **Caracas está en Venezuela** is "Caracas is in Venezuela"). Remember, though, that **estar** is not always used when talking about location, because **ser** is used to tell where someone is from (e.g., **Leo y Sofía son de Panamá, pero Ana es de Chile** is "Leo and Sofía are from Panama, but Ana is from Chile"). To identify someone or something, the verb **ser** is used (e.g., **¿Quién es?** is "Who is it?"; **¿Quiénes son las mujeres en el teatro**? is "Who are the women in the theater?").

Ways to Learn New Vocabulary

Being able to acquire and use new vocabulary is one of the major challenges when learning a language. For that reason, you should try different techniques to learn new words in order to determine which approach works best for you.

Some learners will find that listening to the audio glossary a number of times for each lesson will best help them remember new vocabulary. At first, you should simply repeat the Spanish word for the given English word. With time and practice, you should be able to say the Spanish word for the given English word before hearing it.

Making and using flashcards is another approach to learning new vocabulary that works for many learners. The physical act of writing English on one side of the card and Spanish on the other can help you remember new words, and writing words in Spanish helps you remember proper spelling. Including a connector, or bridge word, on the Spanish side of the card can help make it easier to remember new words in Spanish. Consider the case of the verb **correr**, which means "to run." As you think about "to run," you might imagine a student running down a corridor in school. So, on one side of the card you write, "to run," and on the other you write correr in the middle of the card and "**corridor**" in the upper-left corner. As you practice with the word, you start with the English "to run," which makes you think of "**corridor**," which reminds you of correr. The connector can be a word, an image, or anything else that helps you make a connection between the English and Spanish words. One additional advantage of making flashcards is that they allow others to help you learn vocabulary. If you have friends or family members interested in helping you improve your Spanish, ask them to quiz you on your flashcards.

Actividades / Activities

a. Responde de manera afirmativa a las siguientes preguntas utilizando la construcción ir + a + infinitivo. / Answer the following questions affirmatively using the construction ir + a + infinitive.

1. ¿Vas a leer los libros mañana? _____.

2. ¿Vais a llamar por teléfono a vuestro hermano? _____.

3. ¿Va a ir al cine Fernando con sus amigos? _____.

4. ¿Va a tomar café Elena a las tres de la tarde?_____.

5. ¿Tus amigos y tú van a bailar en el club? _____.

6. ¿Tus vecinos van a ir al teatro mañana? _____.

b. Esteban y Luisa quieren ir de vacaciones con sus hijos Felipe y Elena, pero no saben adónde ir. / Esteban and Luisa want to go on vacation with their children Felipe and Elena, but they don't know where to go.

Lee el siguiente diálogo y contesta las preguntas. / Read the following dialogue and answer the questions.

Esteban: ¡Vamos de vacaciones a Puerto Rico!

Luisa: No quiero [I don't want] ir a Puerto Rico. ¿Por qué no vamos a Ecuador?

Felipe: No, mami, Ecuador está muy lejos [far]. Vamos a México.

Elena: Prefiero [I prefer] ir a la República Dominicana.

Luisa: Yo creo que [that] México es una buena idea.

Felipe: ¡Sí, mami, México es una buena idea!

Esteban: ¡Está bien! Vamos a México.

Elena: OK, en un año [year], vamos a la República Dominicana. ¿Está bien?

Esteban: No, Elena, es mucho dinero [money]. Solo vamos a ir a México para nuestras vacaciones. En dos años, vamos a la República Dominicana, ¿OK?

Elena: Papi y mami, ¿pueden [can they] ir con nosotros mis amigas Rebeca y Alicia?

Luisa: No, Elena, este es un viaje [trip] de familia, no de amigos.

Esteban: ¿Y cuándo debemos ir a México? ¿La próxima semana [next week] o en cuatro semanas?

Felipe: Yo quiero ir la próxima semana.

Elena: Yo quiero ir en cuatro semanas porque voy a tener [to have] las vacaciones de la universidad.

Esteban: OK, ¡vamos a México en cuatro semanas!

1. ¿Adónde va de vacaciones la familia Quirós Sánchez? _____.

2. ¿Qué cree Luisa de la posibilidad de ir a México? _____.

3. ¿Por qué Esteban no quiere [doesn't want] ir a la República Dominicana en un año? _____.

4. ¿Cuándo va la familia a México? _____.

5. ¿Van a ir de vacaciones las amigas de Elena con la familia Quirós Sánchez? _____.

6. ¿Cuándo va la familia a la República Dominicana? _____.

c. ¡Ahora es tu turno! Completa las siguientes preguntas. / Now it's your turn! Complete the following answers.

1. ¿Cuándo van de vacaciones tú y tu familia?_____
en cinco días.

2. ¿Adónde van ustedes? _____
Chile.

3. ¿Quién es tu futbolista favorito? _____ Lionel Messi de Argentina.

4. ¿Dónde estudia español Ana? _____
en su casa.

5. ¿Con quiénes vas al cine y al teatro? _____
mis amigos.

6. ¿Por qué viaja Roberto mucho a Panamá? _____
sus abuelos viven en Panamá.

d. De las siguientes frases, escoge la opción más apropiada. / From the following sentences, choose the most appropriate option.

1. Javier y Erica _____ salsa y merengue en el club.

a) bailar b) bailamos c) bailan

2. La familia Quirós García va a _____ México el próximo mes.

a) visitar b) visitan c) visitáis

3. Cecilia _____ con su madre todos [every] los días.

a) hablan b) habla c) hablar

4. Alejandra _____ el café todas las mañanas.

a) preparan b) preparáis c) prepara

5. Yo _____ la radio en mi carro.

a) escucho b) escuchas c) escuchamos

6. Guillermo _____ diez horas al día.

a) trabajar b) trabaja c) trabajas

7. Manuel, Sandra y yo _____ español a las cuatro de la tarde.

a) estudiáis b) estudian c) estudiamos

8. Leonor _____ a casa a las seis de la tarde.

a) llegas b) llega c) llegar

9. Yo _____ a _____ al supermercado.

a) voy...ir b) ir...voy c) ir...vas

10. Vosotros _____ a _____ karaoke en el bar.

a) van...cantar b) vais...cantar c) vamos...cantar

Respuestas correctas / Correct Answers

a. 1. Sí, voy a leer los libros mañana.

2. Sí, vamos a llamar por teléfono a nuestro hermano.

3. Sí, Fernando va a ir al cine con sus amigos.

4. Sí, Elena va a tomar café a las tres de la tarde.

5. Sí, mis amigos y yo vamos a bailar en el club.

6. Sí, mis vecinos van a ir al teatro mañana.

b. 1. La familia Quirós Sánchez va de vacaciones a México.

2. Luisa cree que México es una buena idea.

3. Esteban no quiere ir a la República Dominicana en un año porque es mucho dinero.

4. La familia va a México en cuatro semanas.

5. No, las amigas de Elena no van a ir de vacaciones con la familia Quirós Sánchez.

6. La familia va a la República Dominicana en dos años.

c. 1. Vamos de vacaciones en cinco días.

2. Vamos a Chile.

3. Mi futbolista favorito es Lionel Messi de Argentina.

4. Ana estudia español en su casa.

5. Voy al cine y al teatro con mis amigos.

6. Roberto viaja mucho a Panamá porque sus abuelos viven en Panamá.

d. 1. c) bailan   6. b) trabaja

2. a) visitar   7. c) estudiamos

3. b) habla   8. b) llega

4. c) prepara   9. a) voy…ir

5. a) escucho   10. b) vais…cantar

Expressing Time in Spanish

Vocabulario nuevo / New Vocabulary

el presente – present	**la semana** – week
el tiempo – time, weather	**el fin de semana** – weekend
el segundo – second	**el mes** – month
el minuto – minute	**el año** – year
la hora – hour, time	**antes de** – before
hoy – today	**después de** – after
¿Qué hora es? – What time is it?	**la tarde** – afternoon
el cuarto – quarter	**por la tarde** – in the afternoon
la media (hora) – half an hour	**la noche** – night
en punto – on the dot, exactly	**por la noche** – at night
Son las tres. – It's three o'clock	**la fecha** – date
a las cinco – at five o'clock	**¿Cuál es la fecha de hoy?** – What is today's date?
el mediodía – noon	**la celebración** – celebration
la medianoche – midnight	**el cumpleaños** – birthday
la mañana – morning	**el Año Nuevo** – New Year's Day
por la mañana – in the morning	**la Navidad** – Christmas
No entiendo. – I don't understand. **¿Entiendes?** – Do you understand? [informal, singular]	**¿Qué quiere decir?** – What does it mean?
lunes – Monday	**viernes** – Friday
martes – Tuesday	**sábado** – Saturday
miércoles – Wednesday	**domingo** – Sunday
jueves – Thursday	
enero – January	**julio** – July
febrero – February	**agosto** – August

marzo – March **abril** – April **mayo** – May **junio** – June	**septiembre** – September **octubre** – October **noviembre** – November **diciembre** – December
la estación – season **la primavera**–spring **el verano** – summer	**el otoño** – autumn **el invierno** – winter

Repaso general / General Review

Telling Time

The verb ser is always used to talk about time. "What time is it?" is ¿Qué hora es?, and the answer to this question almost always begins with son las (e.g., Son las dos is "It's two o'clock"). To express minutes after an hour, y is used; to express minutes before an hour, menos is used (e.g., Son las tres y diez is "It's ten minutes after three"; Son las ocho menos veinte is "It's twenty minutes before eight"). Cuarto means "quarter" and media means "half," so "It's quarter to eleven" is Son las once menos cuarto, and "It's five thirty" is Son las cinco y media. Es is used instead of son when it's one o'clock, noon, or midnight (e.g., Es la una; Es mediodía; Es medianoche). To say "at" a certain time, use a las or a la (e.g., La clase termina a las cuatro is "The class ends at four o'clock"). When talking about time of day in general, por is used, but when talking about a specific time, de is used (e.g., "We study in the afternoon" is Estudiamos por la tarde; "They eat at eight thirty in the morning" is Comen a las ocho y media de la mañana).

Days, Months, and the Date

Monday, which is lunes, is the first day of the week in the Spanish-speaking world. The definite article is used to express the idea of "on a certain day or days" (e.g., El viernes hay clase is "There is class on

Friday"; Los domingos no trabajo is "On Sundays I don't work"). "January" in Spanish is enero; the other 11 months in Spanish are cognates with the months in English. Although names of people and places are capitalized in Spanish (e.g., Carmen González, Paraguay), days of the week, months of the year, nationalities, names of languages, and names of religions are not capitalized in Spanish (e.g., lunes, febrero, cubano, inglés, católicas).

"What is today's date?" is ¿Cuál es la fecha de hoy?. The answer to this question is, for example, Es el veintidós de marzo, which is "It's March twenty-second." Spanish typically uses cardinal numbers for the date (e.g., Es el tres de noviembre; Es el once de agosto), except when it's the first, for which Spanish speakers often use primero (e.g., "It's the first of June" is Es el primero de junio). When saying today's date, the definite article el is not needed (e.g., "Today is the seventeenth of May" is Hoy es diecisiete de mayo).

Improving Your Spoken Spanish

One way to improve your ability to speak Spanish is to listen and repeat what is being said by a newscaster either on the radio or on television. Newscasters tend to speak slowly and clearly, offering beginning language learners the chance to repeat what they hear. This exercise is really about getting used to saying things in Spanish and much less about understanding it, because beginning language learners will understand only some of what is said in the news. Still, this repetition of Spanish is a valuable exercise to help you get used to making the sounds of spoken Spanish. And this activity will be helpful in improving your ability to pronounce words in Spanish, because if you limit yourself to saying only things you understand perfectly well, you won't actually be speaking much Spanish.

Understanding Spoken Spanish Better

If you don't understand what someone is saying, you might say No entiendo, which is "I don't understand." To say "Do you understand?," you would say ¿Entiendes? (which is the informal, singular form) or ¿Entiende? (which is the formal, singular form). ¿Qué quiere decir...? means "What does...mean? (e.g., ¿Qué quiere decir fecha? is "What does fecha mean?"). Using these expressions when speaking Spanish will help you understand more of what is being said to you.

Actividades / Activities

a. Contesta las siguientes preguntas. / Answer the following questions.

1. ¿Cuál es la fecha del día de San Valentín? _____.

2. ¿Cuál es la fecha del día de San Patricio? _____.

3. ¿Cuál es la fecha del día de la independencia [independence] de los Estados Unidos? _____.

4. ¿Cuál es la fecha del día después del Año Nuevo?_____.

5. La Noche Buena es la noche antes de la Navidad. ¿Cuál es la fecha de la Noche Buena? _____.

6. ¿Cuándo es el Día de Acción de Gracias [Thanksgiving] _____.

b. Javier le está explicando a su nieta Diana los meses del año. ¿Puedes ayudarle a Javier? / Javier is explaining to his granddaughter Diana the months of the year. Can you help Javier?

Los meses del año son: / The months of the year are:

1. e_____   7. j _____

2. f_____   8. a _____

3. m _____   9. s _____

4. a _____   10. o _____

5. m _____   11. n _____

6. j _____   12. d _____

c. Diego es estudiante de maestría en negocios y les está explicando a sus padres Luis y Cecilia su horario para este semestre en la universidad. / Diego is a master's degree student in business, and he is explaining to his parents Luis and Cecilia his schedule for this semester at the university.

Completa el diálogo con la información necesaria. / Complete the dialogue with the necessary information.

Diego: Este semestre tengo [I have] clases los lunes [on Mondays] de (5:30 pm)

1. _____ a (7:45 pm) 2. _____. Los martes tengo

clases al (12:00 pm) 3. _____ y después a (4:15 pm) 4. _____.

Los miércoles no tengo clases, pero siempre [always] hay una reunión a (6:25 pm)

5. _____ en la cafetería [cafeteria]. Los jueves voy a clases a (8:00

am) 6. _____ y a (9:55 am) 7. _____. A (1:00 pm)

8. _____ voy a la biblioteca. Estoy muy contento porque los viernes no voy a la

universidad. Bueno [Well], ¿qué hora es?

Cecilia: Son 9. (7:50) _____.

Diego: ¡Oh no, necesito ir a la universidad! ¡Adiós!

d. La abuela de Diana le compró un reloj muy bonito. Diana está aprendiendo a usar el reloj. / Diana's grandmother bought her a very nice watch. Diana is learning how to use it.

¿Puedes ayudarle a Diana? / Can you help Diana?

1. Cecilia: Diana, ¿qué hora es? _____

2. Cecilia: Diana, ¿qué hora es? _____

3. Cecilia: Diana, ¿qué hora es? _____

4. Cecilia: Diana, ¿qué hora es? _____

5. Cecilia: Diana, ¿qué hora es? _____

e. Pablo es estudiante de la universidad, y Marisol es estudiante de secundaria. Ellos son hermanos, y están hablando sobre sus planes para esta semana. / Pablo is a college student, and Marisol is a high school student. They are siblings, and they are talking about their plans for this week.

Completa la información con las respuestas más lógicas. / Complete the information with the most logical answers.

1. Pablo: Los lunes tengo un examen de español _____

a) a la una de la tarde b) a media noche c) a las tres de la mañana

2. Marisol: Los lunes voy al gimnasio [gymnasium] _____

a) justo [just] antes de las dos de la mañana b) al mediodía c) a media noche

3. Pablo: Yo también [also] voy al gimnasio, pero _____

a) a las tres y media de la mañana b) por la mañana c) a las once y media de la noche

4. Marisol: Los jueves tengo mi laboratorio [laboratory] de biología [biology] ____

a) por la tarde b) a la una de la mañana c) a las once de la noche

5. Pablo: Los viernes _____ voy con [with] Guillermo al bar [bar].

a) a las nueve de la noche b) a las siete de la mañana c) antes de nuestras clases

6. Marisol: Los sábados _____ Victoria y yo bailamos y cantamos.

a) en nuestra clase de biología b) en un bar popular c) en el mercado

Respuestas correctas / Correct Answers

a. 1. Es el catorce de febrero.

4. Es el dos de enero.

2. Es el diecisiete de marzo.

5. Es el veinticuatro de diciembre.

3. Es el cuatro de julio.

6. Es el cuarto [the fourth] jueves de noviembre.

b. 1. enero   7. julio

2. febrero   8. agosto

3. marzo   9. septiembre

4. abril   10. octubre

5. mayo   11. noviembre

6. junio   12. diciembre

c. 1. las cinco y media de la tarde / las cinco y treinta de la tarde

2. las ocho menos cuarto / las siete y cuarenta y cinco

3. mediodía

4. las cuatro y cuarto de la tarde / las cuatro y quince de la tarde

5. las seis y veinticinco de la tarde

6. las ocho de la mañana

7. las diez menos cinco de la mañana / las nueve y cincuenta y cinco de la mañana

8. la una de la tarde

9. las ocho menos diez / las siete y cincuenta

d. 1. Son las diez y diez.

2. Son las cuatro menos trece. / Son las dos y cuarenta y siete.

3. Es la una y veinticuatro.

4. Son las doce y treinta y ocho.

5. Son las once menos dos. / Son las diez y cincuenta y ocho.

e. 1. a) a la una de la tarde   4. a) por la tarde

2. b) al mediodía   5. a) a las nueve de la noche

3. b) por la mañana   6. b) en un bar popular

Expressions Using the Verb Tener

Vocabulario nuevo / New Vocabulary

el número – number **la característica** – characteristic **la expresión** – expression	**el estudio** – study **la capital** – capital city **el periódico** – newspaper
tener – to have **tener frío** – to be cold **tener calor** – to be hot **tener hambre** – to be hungry **tener sueño** – to be tired **tener prisa** – to be in a hurry **tener ganas de** – to feel like doing **something**	**tener razón** – to be right **tener miedo** – to be afraid **tener cuidado** – to be careful **tener suerte** – to be lucky **tener treinta años** – to be thirty years old **tener éxito** – to be successful
muerto – dead **único** – only, unique **fácil** – easy	**difícil** – difficult **finalmente** – finally **otro** – other, another
la suegra – mother-in-law **el suegro** – father-in-law **la cuñada** – sister-in-law **el cuñado** – brother-in-law **la nuera** – daughter-in-law **el yerno** – son-in-law **la madrastra** – stepmother **el padrastro** – stepfather	**la hijastra** – stepdaughter **el hijastro** – stepson **la hermanastra** – stepsister **el hermanastro** – stepbrother **el medio hermano** – half brother **el bisabuelo** – great-grandfather **la bisnieta** – great-granddaughter **el gemelo** – twin

Repaso general / General Review

The Verb tener

One of the most commonly used verbs in Spanish is tener, which means "to have." In many cases, tener is used as it is in English (e.g., Tenemos muchas sobrinas is "We have many nieces"). The present tense endings for tener are regular -er endings, but there is a g in the yo form and an ie in the stem of the tú, usted, and ustedes forms. The conjugation of tener is as follows.

tener [to have]

tengo	tenemos
tienes	tenéis
tiene	tienen

Expressions with tener

The verb tener is used with a number of different expressions in Spanish. Some of these expressions describe physical conditions (e.g., tener frío is "to be cold"; tener hambre is "to be hungry"), while others describe emotional conditions or situations (e.g., tener miedo is "to be afraid"; tener razón is "to be right"). Among the most commonly used tener expressions are tener que + infinitive [to have to do something] and tener ganas de + infinitive [to feel like doing something] (e.g., Tengo que hablar con mi suegro is "I have to speak with my father-in-law"; ¿Tienes ganas de ir al teatro? is "Do you feel like going to the theater?").

Estar: Showing the Result of an Action

One way estar is used is to show the result of a previous action. This use of estar can be seen, for example, with the verbs morir [to die] and abrir [to open] (e.g., Mi abuelo está muerto is "My grandfather is dead"; Las puertas están abiertas is "The doors are open").

Characteristics of Successful Language Learners

Improving skills in a second language results form staying motivated and developing good learning habits. Language learners make the most progress when studying the language becomes important to them—important enough to practice consistently, important enough to be comfortable making mistakes, and important enough to accept that achieving proficiency takes considerable time and effort. In fact, studying a second language shares much in common with playing a sport or a musical instrument. Some of it's about knowing what to do, but much more of it is practicing so that what you do becomes natural, even automatic.

Successful language learners most often have some real-world connection to the language, such as a desire to travel, a job situation, or a relationship that gives them a personal stake in being able to communicate in another language. There are so many Spanish speakers in the United States right now that, if you look for them, you should be able to find opportunities to communicate in the language. It also helps to be interested not only in the language, but also in the culture and history of the Spanish-speaking world. Practice often, make mistakes, and have some fun. Your Spanish proficiency is sure to improve as long as learning Spanish is important to you.

When to Use the Dictionary

As a beginning language learner, you will certainly encounter words in Spanish you don't understand, so you should consult a dictionary from time to time. Be careful, however, not to use the dictionary too much. Because there are many words you won't recognize when you read them, you might be tempted to look up any words you don't understand. But using the dictionary too much results in reduced reading comprehension, because going back and forth to the dictionary so often means that you lose the point of the text you're reading.

One way to think about when to use the dictionary is the following: You should only use the dictionary when you're angry. This means that you should use the dictionary when you come across a word that you have seen so much—and you still don't know what it means—that it makes you angry. Using the dictionary only when you're angry means that you'll be looking up the most important words—the ones you come across often in your reading.

Improving Your Reading Skills

If you make it a habit to begin each day by reading the news in Spanish on the Internet, you will improve your reading skills while you find out what's happening in the world. Accept that you're not going to understand everything you read, and that's okay. Your purpose with this reading is not to understand every word but, rather, to read in Spanish to get a general sense of what's going on in the world of politics, sports, entertainment, or whatever specific topic interests you. Accepting less-than-perfect reading comprehension is like being willing to make mistakes in conversation. Dive in and do your best; with time and practice, improved reading proficiency will follow.

Two popular websites with news from the United States are CNN en Español and Fox News Latino (as long as you look at the version in Spanish). For news from Mexico, you might consult the website for the newspaper El Universal. One good place to get news from Spain is the website for the newspaper El País. If you're more interested in what's happening in some other country, do a Google search using the word periódico [newspaper] and the name of the country that interests you.

Actividades / Activities

a. Contesta las siguientes preguntas usando el verbo tener. Nota: Necesitas consultar la información de las familias del vecindario al inicio del cuaderno. / Answer the following questions using the verb tener. / Note: You need to consult the information about the neighborhood families at the beginning of the workbook.

1. ¿Cuántos hermanos tiene Elena? _____ .

2. ¿Cuántas hermanos tiene Pablo? _____ .

3. ¿Cuántos hijos tienen Luis y Cecilia? _____ .

4. ¿Cuántos tíos tienen Mariana y Diana? _____ .

5. ¿Cuántos hermanos tiene una hija única? _____ .

6. ¿Cuántos años tiene en 2020 una persona que nació [who was born] en 1995? _____ .

b. Javier y Erica tienen dos hijas: Diana de cuatro años y Mariana de un año. Erica está embarazada otra vez, y todos están muy felices. Erica y Javier están hablando sobre sus hijas y los planes para hoy. / Javier and Erica have two daughters: Diana, who is four years old, and Mariana, who is one. Erica is pregnant again, and everyone is very happy. Erica and Javier are talking about their daughters and the plans for today.

Completa el siguiente diálogo utilizando tener que y/o tener ganas de. Tienes que conjugar tener de manera correcta. / Complete the following dialogue using tener que and/or tener ganas de. You have to conjugate tener correctly.

Erica: Hoy (yo) 1. _____ llevar a las niñas [girls] al parque. Ellas necesitan estar con [with] otros niños [children].

Javier: Sí, es una buena idea.

Erica: También, 2. _____ ir al supermercado porque no tenemos pañales [diapers] para Mariana. 3. _____ comprar suficientes [enough] para el fin de semana.

Javier: 4. _____ invitar [to inv Erica: ¡Sí, por supuesto [of course]! Pero el viernes Diana 5. _____ ir al dentista a las 4:00.

Nosotras vamos a regresar a casa [go home] a las 5:30.

Javier: 6. _____ hablar con mis padres para pedirles que lleguen [ask them to arrive] a las 7:00.

Erica: 7. _____ comer dos postres [dessert] diferentes. ¿Cuáles?

Erica: Diana solo 8. _____ comer helado [ice cream], pero yo quiero un pastel [cake].

Javier: Podemos [We can] comer un pastel y helado.

Erica: ¡OK! 9. (Yo) _____ hablar con tu madre. En la noche, ella puede cantarle una canción

[song] a Diana porque ella tiene miedo de la oscuridad [dark].

c. Completa las siguientes frases utilizando expresiones con tener. / Complete the following sentences using expressions with tener.

tener sueño   tener hambre   tener miedo   tener éxito

tener suerte   tener ___ años   tener frío   tener prisa

1. Son las 2:45 de la tarde y Alberto no ha comido nada [hasn't eaten anything] hoy. Alberto _____.

2. Alberto tiene muchos pacientes (patients) todos los días. Él _____ como [as] dentista.

3. Son las 7:50 de la mañana, pero Diego tiene clase a las 8:00. El _____ para llegar a la universidad.

4. Donde [Where] yo vivo, hay posibilidad de huracanes [hurricanes] de junio a noviembre. Nosotros siempre _____ en esos [those] meses.

5. Generalmente [Generally], Diego no estudia para sus exámenes, pero sus notas [grades] son muy buenas. Él _____.

6. Luis trabaja mucho por la noche y solo duerme [sleeps] cinco horas. Él _____.

7. Diana, la nieta de Luis y Cecilia, _____ cuatro

_____.

8. Pablo y Marisol están en un bar con aire acondicionado [air conditioning] muy fuerte.

Ellos _____.

d. Luis y Cecilia van a cenar en la casa de su hijo. / Luis and Cecilia are going to have dinner at their son's house.

Lee el siguiente diálogo y contesta las preguntas. / Read the following dialogue and answer the questions.

Luis: Vamos a ir a la casa de Javier y Erica a las siete porque Diana tiene una cita [appointment] con el dentista. ¿Quieres llevar algo [something] para la cena?

Cecilia: Si, quiero preparar un postre [dessert]. Voy a preparar tres leches, pero tengo que ir al supermercado por los ingredientes [ingredients].

Luis: Tengo que llamar a un cliente [client] antes de ir al supermercado.

Cecilia: OK. Vamos a las cinco menos cuarto.

Luis: ¡Está bien! Tengo que leer mi correo electrónico [e-mail] y llamar a la oficina.

Cecilia: Yo también tengo que leer mi correo electrónico, pero no tengo que llamar a la oficina.

Luis: Tengo ganas de llevar mi guitarra [guitar] para cantarles a las niñas.

Cecilia: ¡Qué bien! Yo también [also] quiero [I want] cantar.

1. ¿Qué prepara Cecilia para la cena? _____.

2. ¿Por qué Cecilia tiene que ir al supermercado? _____.

3. ¿Qué va a llevar Luis a la casa de su hijo? _____.

4. ¿Tiene Cecilia que llamar a la oficina? _____.

Lectura cultural / Cultural Reading

Lee el texto siguiente y contesta las preguntas de forma cierto ("C") o falso ("F"). / Read the following text and answer the questions as either true ("C") or false ("F").

Aunque la lengua española es uno de los aspectos que une al mundo hispano, también existen muchas diferencias entre regiones y países. Ahora sabes que hay países, áreas y regiones que pronuncian consonantes y/o palabras de manera diferente. También, hay palabras que en un país tienen un significado diferente que en otro. Hay palabras que solo tienen un uso o significado particular en una región específica, pero no existen en otras. Por ejemplo, "cake" en Argentina se dice torta, en Puerto Rico bizcocho, en España tarta y en México pastel. Otra palabra interesante es "popcorn," que en Colombia se dice crispetas, en Argentina pochoclo y en España palomitas. Además, "bus" en Argentina se dice colectivo, en Cuba y Puerto Rico guagua, en Costa Rica bus y en México camión.

Otra de las diferencias importantes es la correspondiente a la localización del país dependiendo del hemisferio. Los países que están al norte del ecuador tienen diferentes estaciones que los países al sur del ecuador. Cuando es el verano para los países en el hemisferio norte, es el invierno para los países del hemisferio sur. Otros países solo tienen una temporada seca y una temporada de lluvia, pero no tienen cuatro estaciones como los Estados Unidos, por ejemplo.

Otro de los contrastes entre los países hispanos son los días feriados. Aunque muchos países tienen los mismos días feriados, no todos hacen las mismas celebraciones. Estas celebraciones van a ser diferentes dependiendo del país y las regiones dentro de cada país. Esto se debe a que cada país tiene su propia cultura y costumbres. Los días feriados pueden ser nacionales o regionales, y muchas veces las celebraciones regionales dependen de creencias religiosas y de los personajes santos asociados a una región.

En cuanto al Día de la Independencia, Guatemala, El Salvador, Costa Rica, Honduras y Nicaragua lo celebran cada año el 15 de septiembre, mientras que México lo celebra el 16 de septiembre y Chile el 18 de ese mes. En agosto esta celebración la tienen Ecuador, Bolivia y Uruguay. En el mes de julio, se celebra el Día de la Independencia para Venezuela, Argentina, Colombia y Perú. Por supuesto, este día es una celebración muy importante en cada país y tiene sus orígenes en la historia independentista de España.

No se puede negar la influencia de España en Hispanoamérica, y en cuanto a uno de los feriados importantes para las familias se encuentra el Día de los Reyes Magos, que se celebra el seis de enero o la medianoche del cinco de enero. La idea general y tradicional es que los Reyes Magos—Melchor, Gaspar y Baltasar—les llevan regalos a los niños. Esta celebración es común en muchos de los países hispanohablantes.

1. "Cake" en México es bizcocho.

_____

2. "Bus" se dice [is said] igual [the same] en todos los países de Hispanoamérica. _____

3. Todos los países en Hispanoamérica tienen cuatro estaciones como en los Estados Unidos. _____

4. Algunos países tienen una temporada seca y una temporada lluviosa.

_____

5. Cada país en Hispanoamérica tiene su propia cultura y costumbres.

_____

6. Todos los días feriados en Hispanoamérica son feriados nacionales.

_____

Respuestas correctas / Correct Answers

a. 1. Elena tiene dos hermanos: Felipe y Érica.

2. Pablo tiene una hermana: Marisol.

3. Luis y Cecilia tienen tres hijos: Alberto, Diego y Javier.

4. Mariana y Diana tienen tres tíos—Alberto, Diego y Felipe—y una tía: Elena.

5. Una hija única no tiene hermanos.

6. La persona tiene veinticinco años.

b. 1. tengo ganas de

2. tengo que

3. Tengo que

4. Tengo ganas de

5. tiene que

6. Tengo que / Tenemos que

7. Tengo ganas de

8. tiene ganas de

9. Tengo que / Tengo ganas de

c. 1. tiene hambre

5. tiene suerte

2. tiene éxito   6. tiene sueño

3. tiene prisa   7. tiene cuatro años

4. tenemos miedo   8. tienen frío

d. 1. Cecilia prepara un postre: tres leches [a sponge cake soaked in three kinds of milk].

2. Cecilia tiene que comprar ingredientes para el postre.

3. Luis va a llevar una guitarra a la casa de su hijo.

4. No, Cecilia no tiene que llamar a la oficina.

Lectura cultural

1. F   2. F   3. F   4. C   5. C

6. F

Although the Spanish language is one of the aspects that unites the Hispanic world, there are also many differences between regions and countries. You now know that there are countries, areas, and regions that pronounce consonants and/or words in different ways. There are also words that have a different meaning in one country than in another. There are words that only have one use or particular meaning in a specific region but that don't exist in others. For example, "cake" in Argentina is torta, in Puerto Rico bizcocho, in Spain tarta, and in

Mexico pastel. Another interesting word is "popcorn," which in Colombia is crispetas, in Argentina pochoclo, and in Spain palomitas. Moreover, "bus" is colectivo in Argentina, guagua in Cuba and Puerto Rico, bus in Costa Rica, and camión in Mexico.

Another of the important differences relates to the location of the country, depending on its hemisphere. The countries that are north of the equator have different seasons than the countries to the south of the equator. When it's summer for the countries in the northern hemisphere, it's winter for the countries of the southern hemisphere. Other countries only have a dry season and a rainy season, but don't have four seasons, as in, for example, the United States.

Holidays are another of the contrasts among Hispanic countries. Although many countries have the same holidays, not all celebrate them the same way. These celebrations will be different depending on the country and the regions within each country. This is due to each country having its own culture and customs. Holidays can be national or regional, and often the regional celebrations depend on the religious beliefs and the saints associated with a region.

As for Independence Day, Guatemala, El Salvador, Costa Rica, Honduras, and Nicaragua celebrate it each year on September 15th, while Mexico celebrates it on September 16th, and Chile celebrates it on September 18th. It's celebrated in August in Ecuador, Bolivia, and Uruguay. Independence Day is celebrated in July in Venezuela, Argentina, Colombia, and Perú. This day is, of course, a very important celebration in each country and has its origins in the history of independence from Spain.

The influence of Spain on Spanish America cannot be denied, and among the more important holidays for families is Epiphany [The Day of the Wise Men], which is celebrated on January 6th or at midnight on January 5th. The general and traditional idea is that the Wise Men—Melchior, Gaspar, and Balthasar—bring gifts to children. This celebration is common in many of the Spanish-speaking countries.

Verbs like Hacer and Interrogative Words

Vocabulario nuevo / New Vocabulary

hacer – to make, to do **poner** – to put hacer **salir** – to leave, to go out **traer** – to bring hacer **explicar** – to explain	**ganar** – to win, to earn **ejercicio** – to exercise **hacer una pregunta** – to ask a question **una fiesta** – to throw a party
¿Cómo está Carla? – How is Carla?	**¿Cómo es Carla?** – What is Carla like?
el ejercicio – exercise **la fiesta** – party	**la cama** – bed **la radio** – radio
la temperatura – temperature **los grados** – degrees	**el huracán** – hurricane **la precipitación** – precipitation
¿Qué tiempo hace? – What's the weather like? **Hace buen tiempo.** – It's good weather. **Hace mal tiempo.** – It's bad weather. **Hace sol.** – It's sunny. **Hace viento.** – It's windy. **Hace frío.** – It's cold. **Hace calor.** – It's hot. **Hace fresco.** – It's cool. Llovizna. – It's drizzling. **Está a veinticinco grados.** – It's twenty-five degrees.	**Truena.** – It's thundering. **Está nublado.** – It's cloudy. **Está despejado.** – It's clear (cloudless). **Llueve.** – It's raining. **Está lloviendo.** – It's raining. **la lluvia** – rain **Hay niebla.** – It's foggy. **Llovizna.** – It's drizzling. **Nieva.** – It's snowing. **Hay hielo.** – It's icy. **Caen rayos.** – It's lightning. **Hay tormenta.** – There's a storm.

la puntuación – punctuation **el signo de puntuación** – punctuation mark **el punto** – period, point **dos puntos** – colon	**el punto y coma** – semicolon **los signos de interrogación** – question marks **los signos de exclamación** – exclamation marks **si** – if **la coma** – comma

Repaso general / General Review

Hacer and Expressions with hacer

The verb hacer means "to make" or "to do," and it's one of the most commonly used verbs in Spanish. Beyond its normal use (e.g., "I always do my work" is Siempre hago mi trabajo), hacer is used in a number of expressions, such as hacer una pregunta, which is "to ask a question," and hacer una fiesta, which is "to throw a party." Hacer is also used with many of the weather expressions (e.g., ¿Qué tiempo hace? is "What is the weather like?"; Hace sol is "It's sunny"; Hace mal tiempo is "It's bad weather"). If you consult the website of Spain's Agencia Estatal de Meteorología [State Meteorological Agency], at aemet.es, you can see a meteorologist giving a weather report. All present tense endings for hacer are regular; the only unusual form of the verb is the yo form (hago), which has a g.

Verbs Conjugated like hacer

Verbs conjugated like hacer (meaning that they also use regular endings and have a g in the yo form) include poner [to put], salir [to leave, to go out], and traer [to bring]. The yo forms for these verbs are pongo, salgo, and traigo.

Interrogatives

The meaning of cómo is different when used with estar than it is when used with ser because estar expresses a state or condition, while ser expresses an inherent characteristic of someone or something. ¿Cómo están las chicas? asks "How are the girls?" while ¿Cómo son las chicas? asks "What are the girls like?"

The interrogative qué [what] is used directly before a noun (e.g., ¿Qué clases tomas este semestre? is "What classes are you taking this semester?"). The interrogatives cuál and cuáles [which or what] are often used before the preposition de, as in ¿Cuáles de las camas es tu cama?, which is "Which of the beds is your bed?" You use qué when asking for a definition or explanation (e.g., ¿Qué pasa aquí? is "What's happening here?"; ¿Qué significa salir? is "What does salir mean?"). The interrogatives cuál and cuáles are used when you want someone to tell you some information, not explain it (e.g., ¿Cuál es la fecha de hoy? is "What is today's date?"; ¿Cuál es el nombre de la profesora del curso? is "What is the name of the professor of the course?").

Punctuation

In Spanish, it is never correct to put a comma after the second-to-last item in a list (e.g., "I'm going to bring many books, a notebook, and a computer" is Voy a traer muchos libros, un cuaderno y una computadora).

Questions in Spanish begin with an inverted question mark, which could be at the start of a sentence or at the start of a clause in the middle of a sentence (e.g., ¿Dónde están las camas? is "Where are the beds?"; Si tenemos tiempo, ¿debemos salir después de la clase? is "If we have time, should we go out after the class?"). An exclamation must begin with an inverted exclamation mark and end with an exclamation mark (e.g., ¡Que día fantástico! is "What a fantastic day!"; Después del examen, ¡qué fiesta vamos a hacer! is "After the exam, what a party we're going to throw!").

Actividades / Activities

a. Contesta las siguientes preguntas sobre el pronóstico del tiempo en Buenos Aires y Guadalajara. / Answer the following questions about the weather forecast in Buenos Aires and Guadalajara.

Buenos Aires, Argentina			Guadalajara, México		
hoy	mañana	domingo	hoy	mañana	domingo
31°	31°	32°	41°	41°	33°
Soleado	Parcialmente nublado	Parcialmente nublado	Soleado	Parcialmente nublado	Tormenta
18°	18°	18°	25°	26°	21°
Temperatura mínima	Temperatura mínima	Temperatura mínima	Temperatura mínima	Temperatura mínima	Temperatura mínima
0%	0%	0%	0%	0%	80%
Probabilidad de lluvia	Probabilidad de lluvia	Probabilidad de lluvia	Probabilidad de lluvia	Probablidad de lluvia	Probabilidad de lluvia

1. ¿Cuándo y dónde hay probabilidad de lluvia? _____

2. ¿Cuál es la temperatura mínima en Buenos Aires el domingo? _____ .

3. ¿Cuál es la temperatura máxima el viernes en Buenos Aires?

_____ .

4. ¿Cuál es la probabilidad de lluvia en Buenos Aires el sábado? _____ .

5. ¿Cuándo y dónde hay probabilidad de tormenta?

_____ .

6. ¿Qué tiempo hace en Buenos Aires hoy? _____ .

7. ¿Qué tiempo va a hacer en Guadalajara el sábado?

_____ .

8. ¿Cuál es la temperatura máxima de hoy en Guadalajara?

_____ .

9. ¿Cuál es la temperatura mínima el sábado en Guadalajara?

_____ .

b. Diana quiere ir a la piscina de Villa Celeste. Erica va a revisar el pronóstico del tiempo. / Diana wants to go to the pool in Villa Celeste. Erica is going to check the weather forecast.

Lee el siguiente diálogo y contesta las preguntas. / Read the following dialogue and answer the questions.

Diana: ¡Mami, quiero [I want] ir a la piscina!

Erica: Sí, está bien, pero tenemos que llevar a tu hermana Mariana con nosotras.

Diana: Está bien, mami, pero ¡vamos a la piscina!

Erica: Muy bien, pero primero [first] voy a mirar el pronóstico del tiempo.

Erica: Diana, ¿puedes [can you] poner la televisión, por favor?

Diana: ¡Sí, mami!

Erica: Diana, hoy no vamos a ir a la piscina porque va a llover.

Diana: No, mami, ¡hace sol!

Erica: Sí, hace sol ahora, pero en una hora va a llover mucho.

Diana: Pero yo quiero ir a la piscina.

Erica: Yo sé [I know], pero no vamos a salir porque va a llover.

Erica: Mañana sí vamos con tu amiga Valeria, ¿está bien?

Diana: ¡Sí, mañana!

1. ¿Por qué Erica y sus hijas no van hoy a la piscina? _____ .

2. ¿Qué tiempo hace ahora? _____ .

3. ¿Cuándo va a llover? _____ .

4. ¿Cómo se llama la amiga de Diana? _____ .

5. ¿Cuándo van a ir a la piscina? _____ .

c. Completa las frases con la opción apropiada. / Complete the sentences with the appropriate option.

1. Hoy quiero _____ ejercicio a las seis y media de la tarde. Mañana _____ ejercicio con Victoria a las cinco de la tarde.

a) hacemos…hacer b) hacer…vais a hacer c) hacer…voy a hacer

2. ¿Cuál _____ el nombre de tu nuevo vecino?

a) está b) es c) ser

3. ¿Cómo _____ la personalidad [personality] de tu vecino?

a) está b) es c) ser

4. Yo _____ la radio todos los días, pero no _____ la televisión todos los días.

a) pongo…poner b) pongo…ponéis c) pongo…pongo

5. ¿Cuáles _____ los ingredientes [ingredients] que necesitas comprar en el supermercado?

a) están b) eres c) son

6. ¿ _____ vecinos tienes?

a) Cuántos b) Cuántas c) Cuál

7. Marisol y Valeria _____ todos los fines de semana con sus amigos.

a) salgan b) salen c) salimos

8. ¿Y tú? ¿Cuándo _____ con tus amigos?

a) sale b) sales c) salgo

9. ¿Y ustedes? ¿Cuándo _____ los libros para estudiar?

a) traigo b) trae c) traen

d. Escribe la expresión correspondiente a la imagen. / Write the expression corresponding to the image.

Hace frío.   Hace calor.   Hace fresco.

Hace viento.

Está despejado.   Está lloviendo.   Hay niebla.

Nieva.

1. _____

2. _____

3. _____

4. _____

Respuestas correctas / Correct Answers

a. 1. Hay probabilidad de lluvia el domingo en Guadalajara.

2. La temperatura mínima en Buenos Aires el domingo es de 18 grados.

3. La temperatura máxima el viernes en Buenos Aires es de 31 grados.

4. No hay probabilidad de lluvia en Buenos Aires el sábado.

5. Hay probabilidad de tormenta el domingo en Guadalajara.

6. Hoy hace buen tiempo en Buenos Aires. / Hoy en Buenos Aires está soleado. / Hoy en Buenos Aires hace sol.

7. El sábado en Guadalajara va a estar parcialmente nublado.

8. La temperatura máxima de hoy en Guadalajara es de 41 grados.

9. La temperatura mínima el sábado en Guadalajara es de 26 grados.

b. 1. No van a la piscina porque va a llover.   4.

2. Hace sol ahora.

3. Va a llover en una hora.

4. La amiga de Diana se llama Valeria.

5. Van a ir a la piscina mañana.

c. 1. c) hacer…voy a hacer   6. a) Cuántos

2. b) es   7. b) salen

3. b) es   8. b) sales

4. c) pongo…pongo   9. c) traen

5. c) son

d. 1. Hace calor.   3. Está lloviendo.

2. Hace frío.   4. Nieva.

The Verbs Saber and Conocer

Vocabulario nuevo / New Vocabulary

saber – to know facts, to know **how to do something**	**traducir** – to translate
	conducir – to drive
conocer – to know a person	**manejar** – to drive
producir – to produce	**visitar** – to visit
reducir – to reduce	**saludar** – to greet
ofrecer – to offer	**comunicarse** – to communicate
parecer – to seem	
rápido – fast	**que** – that
la respuesta – answer	
con – with	**hacia** – toward
para – for, to, in order to	**hasta** – until
por – for, by, through	**contra** – against
sin – without **since** **entre** – between, among	**desde** – from,
encima de – on top of, over	**cerca de** – near to
sobre – on, about	**lejos de** – far from
debajo de – under	**al lado de** – next to
dentro de – inside of	**a la derecha de** – to the

detrás de – behind	right of
delante de – in front of	**a la izquierda de** – to the left of
enfrente de – across from	**alrededor de** – around, about

Repaso general / General Review

Saber and conocer

Let's approach these verbs by asking the three questions we ask about any new verbs.

1. What do they mean?

2. How do you use them?

3. How do you conjugate them?

What do they mean? Both saber and conocer mean "to know."

How do you use them? The verb saber expresses "to know" in the sense of knowing information or knowing how to do something (e.g., Ellos saben que Marta es simpática is "They know that Marta is nice"; ¿Sabes hablar italiano? is "Do you know how to speak Italian?"). The verb conocer expresses "to know" in the sense of being familiar with someone or with a place or thing (e.g., No conocemos a Arturo is "We don't know Arturo"; Mis amigos conocen una buena biblioteca is "My friends know a good library").

How do you conjugate them? Both saber and conocer have irregular yo forms: yo sé and yo conozco. The other five forms for both verbs are regular.

The Personal a

When the direct object of a verb is a specific person or group of people, the word a must precede the direct object. In the world of grammar, this is called the "personal a," or the a personal in Spanish (e.g., Conozco a Julia, pero no conozco a sus padres is "I know Julia, but I don't know her parents"; ¿A quién buscas? is "Whom are you looking for?"). If the person or group is not specific, no personal a is needed (e.g., Necesitamos unos nuevos amigos is "We need some new friends"). The personal a is generally not used with tener or hay (e.g., Tengo cuatro tíos is "I have four uncles"; Hay un chico al lado de mí is "There's a boy next to me").

Verbs like conocer

The verbs producir [to produce], reducir [to reduce], ofrecer [to offer], parecer [to seem], traducir [to translate], and conducir [to drive] are conjugated like conocer, meaning that they all have a z before the c in the yo form while the other five verb forms in the present are regular.

The present tense of the yo forms for these verbs are produzco, reduzco, ofrezco, parezco, traduzco, and conduzco.

Using en and a

The preposition en [in, at] is used when there is no motion expressed (e.g., Estamos en el parque is "We are in the park"; Ella estudia en la universidad is "She studies at the university"). If what you're talking about involves motion, use the preposition a [to], which is often used with ir [to go] and llegar [to arrive] (e.g., Vamos a la tienda is "We are going to the store"; Siempre llegan a la estación de trenes is "They always arrive at the train station").

Understanding Spoken Spanish

When listening to spoken Spanish, make use of context, cognates, and conjecture. You're more likely to understand what you're hearing if, as the other person is speaking, you focus on context while listening for possible cognates. Conjecture is an opinion or conclusion formed on the basis of incomplete information. When you hear something beyond your current level of comprehension, you must work to make sense of what's being said on the basis of incomplete information because there are gaps in your understanding. Conjecture simply means that at times you should guess what's being said. In fact, what beginning language learners often consider a wild guess is often an informed guess.

Making use of context, cognates, and conjecture will help maximize your understanding of what you hear.

Actividades / Activities

a. Un cliente de Luis Cortés quiere viajar a El Salvador. El cliente le está pidiendo información sobre la ciudad. / A customer of Luis Cortés wants to travel to El Salvador. The customer is asking him for information about the city.

Escoge la respuesta correcta. / Choose the correct answer.

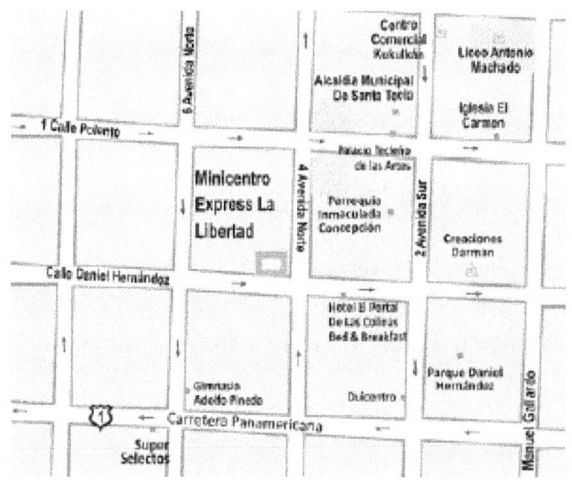

1. ¿Dónde está el Gimnasio [gymnasium] Adolfo Pineda?

a) El gimnasio está en la carretera Panamericana.

b) El gimnasio está entre la 4 Avenida Norte y la carretera Panamericana.

c) El gimnasio está entre la carretera Panamericana y la 2 Avenida Sur.

2. ¿Dónde está la Parroquia Inmaculada Concepción?

a) La parroquia está en el Parque Daniel Hernández.

b) La parroquia está entre la 4 Avenida Norte y la 2 Avenida Sur.

c) La parroquia está en la carretera Panamericana.

3. ¿Dónde está el Hotel El Portal?

a) El hotel está en la 8 Avenida Norte.

b) El hotel está lejos de la Parroquia Inmaculada Concepción.

c) El hotel está cerca del Parque Daniel Hernández.

4. ¿Dónde está el Liceo Antonio Machado?

a) El liceo está detrás de la Iglesia El Carmen.

b) El liceo está al lado del Gimnasio Adolfo Pineda.

c) El liceo está entre la 2 Avenida Sur y la 4 Avenida Norte.

5. ¿Dónde está el Centro Comercial Kukulkán?

a) El centro comercial está lejos del Gimnasio Adolfo Pineda.

b) El centro comercial está en la calle Daniel Hernández.

c) El centro comercial está delante del Minicentro Express La Libertad.

b. El cliente de Luis no sabe exactamente dónde están los países en América Central o América del SSur. / Luis's customer doesn't know exactly where the countries of Central America or South America are located.

Escoge la respuesta correcta. / Choose the correct answer.

1. ¿Dónde está El Salvador?

a) El Salvador está al oeste de México.

b) El Salvador está en América del Norte.

c) El Salvador está al sur de Guatemala.

2. ¿Dónde está Ecuador?

a) Ecuador está cerca de Argentina.

b) Ecuador está entre Bolivia y Paraguay.

c) Ecuador está cerca de Colombia.

3. ¿Dónde está Bolivia?

a) Bolivia está entre Brasil y Chile.

b) Bolivia está cerca de Guatemala.

c) Bolivia está al sur de Paraguay.

4. ¿Dónde está Uruguay?

a) Uruguay está cerca de Perú.

b) Uruguay está al este de Argentina.

c) Uruguay está entre Brasil y Bolivia.

5. ¿Dónde está la República Dominicana?

a) La República Dominicana está oeste de Puerto Rico.

b) La República Dominicana está al oeste de Cuba.

c) La República Dominicana está entre Venezuela y Colombia.

c. Rogelio está buscando trabajo. Hoy tiene una entrevista de trabajo en la agencia de viajes de Luis Cortés. / Rogelio is looking for a job. Today he has a job interview in Luis Cortés's travel agency.

Completa el siguiente diálogo entre Rogelio y Luis. / Complete the following dialogue between Rogelio and Luis Cortés.

Luis: ¡Buenos días, Rogelio! Yo 1. _____ (ser) Luis Cortés.

Rogelio: ¡Mucho gusto, señor Cortés!

Luis: Bueno [Well], Rogelio, ¿usted 2. _____ (tener) experiencia [experience] en otros trabajos?

Rogelio: No, señor. No 3. _____ (tener) experiencia.

Luis: ¿Por qué está buscando trabajo en una agencia de viajes?

Rogelio: 4. _____ (estudiar) administración en turismo y recreación [Tourism and Recreation

Management] y 5. _____ (necesitar) dinero para la universidad.

Luis: ¡Muy bien! 6. ¿_____ (saber) mucho sobre tecnología [technology]?

Rogelio: Sí, señor. 7. _____ (saber) trabajar con Photoshop, y eso [that] es importante

para la publicidad [advertising] en una agencia de viajes.

Luis: Sí, 8. _____ (tener) razón. 9.

¿_____ (saber) organizar

[organize] eventos [events]?

Rogelio: Sí, señor. Yo 10. _____ (saber) organizar eventos. Por ejemplo, yo

11. _____ (organizar) todos los eventos en mi familia. También, yo

12. _____ (ofrecer) muchas fiestas en mi casa.

Luis: 13. ¿_____ (saber) hablar otras lenguas?

Rogelio: Sí, señor. Yo 14. _____ (saber) hablar alemán y francés. Yo

15. _____ (traducir) muchos documentos [documents] para mis amigos.

Luis: 16. ¿_____ (conocer) otros países?

Rogelio: Sí, señor. 17. _____ (conocer) otros países—por ejemplo, España, Francia,

Chile y Panamá.

Luis: ¡Muy bien, Rogelio! ¡Gracias por hablar conmigo [with me]!

d. Escoge la respuesta correcta. No olvides conjugar el verbo. / Choose the correct answer. Don't forget to conjugate the verb.

conocer a saber

1. Esteban y Luisa _____ sus vecinos.

2. Diana no _____ manejar su bicicleta [bicycle].

3. Luis _____ la cuñada de Ana.

4. Luis _____ muchos países de Europa y Asia.

5. Elena no _____ cocinar.

6. Alberto, Diego y Javier _____ jugar [to play] ajedrez [chess].

7. ¿ (Tú) _____ un buen restaurante para ir a comer con tu familia?

8. ¿ (Usted) _____ dónde está la estación de trenes?

9. Yo no _____ una buena universidad para estudiar administración en turismo.

e. Contesta las siguientes preguntas. / Answer the following questions.

entre a la izquierda encima enfrente a la derecha debajo

1. La lámpara está _____ del sillón.

2. El periódico está _____ de la mesa.

3. El televisor está _____ del sillón.

4. El teléfono está _____ la puerta y la ventana.

5. La alfombra está _____ de la mesa.

Respuestas correctas / Correct Answers

a. 1. a)   4. a)

2. b)   5. a)

3. c)

b. 1. c)   4. b)

2. c)   5. a)

3. a)

c. 1. soy   10. sé

2. tiene   11. organizo

3. tengo   12. ofrezco

4. Estudio   13. Sabe

5. necesito   14. sé

6. Sabe   15. traduzco

7. Sé   16. Conoce

8. tiene   17. Conozco

9. Sabe

d. 1. conocen a   6. saben

2. sabe   7. Conoces

3. conoce a   8. Sabe

4. conoce   9. conozco

5. sabe

e. 1. a la derecha   4. entre

2. encima   5. debajo

3. a la derecho

Stem-Changing Verbs

Vocabulario nuevo / New Vocabulary

el cambio – change **la raíz** – root, stem of a verb **la conjugación** – conjugation	**el piano** – piano **el énfasis** – emphasis
sin mí – without me **hacia ti** – toward you **próximo** – next	**contigo** – with you [informal, singular] **conmigo** – with me
comprender – to understand **tocar** – to play an instrument, to touch **pensar** – to think **cerrar** – to close **comenzar** – to begin **empezar** – to begin **entender** – to understand **perder** – to lose **querer** – to want, to love **mentir** – to lie **preferir** – to prefer **encontrar** – to find	**poder** – to be able to **almorzar** – to have lunch **recordar** – to remember **mostrar** – to show **volver** – to return **devolver** – to return something **dormir** – to sleep **morir** – to die **jugar** – to play **servir** – to serve **pedir** – to ask for **repetir** – to repeat

costar – to cost	
¡Qué elegante! – How elegant!	

Repaso general / General Review

Stem-Changing Verbs in the Present

Stem-changing verbs in the present tense have regular endings but change stem in all the singular forms and in the third-person plural form (there is no stem change for the nosotros or vosotros forms). The four possible stem changes are **e à ie, o à ue, e à i,** and **u à ue** (jugar is the only verb with **a u à ue** stem change). Conjugations of stem-changing verbs in the present include the following.

querer [to want, to love]   encontrar [to find]

e - ie   o à-ue

quiero	queremos	encuentro	encontramos
quieres	queréis	encuentras	encontráis
quiere	quieren	encuentra	encuentran

servir [to serve]   jugar [to play]

	e - i		u - ue	
sirvo	servimos		juego	jugamos
sirves	servís		juegas	jugáis
sirve	sirven		juega	juegan

What's easy about stem-changing verbs is remembering that all endings are regular and that the stem change happens only in the boot (in all forms except the nosotros and vosotros forms). What's difficult about stem-changing verbs is remembering which verbs change stem and what the stem change is for each verb.

A commonly used stem-changing verb is costar, meaning "to cost" (e.g., ¿Cuánto cuesta la computadora? is "How much does the computer cost?"; ¿Cuánto cuestan los zapatos? is "How much do the shoes cost?").

Prepositional Pronouns

Pronouns used after a preposition (also known as prepositional pronouns) are the same as the subject pronouns, with two exceptions: The first-person singular form is mí and the second-person singular, informal form is ti. The prepositional pronouns are as follows.

mí	**nosotros, nosotras**
ti	**vosotros, vosotras**

usted	ustedes
él	ellos
ella	ellas

Two forms that are irregular are conmigo, which means "with me," and contigo, which means "with you" (using the informal, singular form of "you").

Knowing Where to Place Spoken Stress

Spanish has three rules that determine where to place the stress in a word when speaking.

1. When a word ends with a vowel or with the letter n or s, you stress the second-to-last syllable (e.g., comen, cervezas, trabajadora).

2. When a word ends with a consonant that is not the letter n or s, you stress the last syllable (e.g., entender, pared, accidental).

3. When a word does not follow the first two rules, an accent mark is used to show which syllable should be stressed (e.g., francés, Ángela, república).

Actividades / Activities

a. Pronunciar cada una de las palabras en esta lista. Para cada palabra, subraya la sílaba acentuada—es decir, la sílaba que lleva énfasis a la hora de hablar. / Pronounce each one of the words on this list. For each word, underline the accented syllable—in other words, the syllable that is emphasized when speaking.

1. chocolate	6. Honduras	11. contigo
2. hospital	7. instrumento	12. lecciones
3. café	8. ciudad	13. dormir
4. universidad	9. veintidós	14. actividad
5. palabra	10. almorzar	15. Málaga

Pablo y sus amigos Sebastián y Guillermo están hablando con Felipe. Ellos quieren convencer a Felipe de ir a la universidad. / Pablo and his friends Sebastián and Guillermo are talking with Felipe. They want to convince Felipe to go to college.

Completa el diálogo con la conjugación correcta del verbo indicado. / Complete the dialogue with the correct conjugation of the indicated verb.

Pablo: Debes tomar clases el próximo semestre [semester].

Felipe: 1. _____ (preferir) tener solo mi trabajo. No 2 _____ (querer).

estresarme [stress out] por las clases y las notas [grades].

Sebastián: Sí, nosotros 3. _____ (saber) que no quieres estresarte, pero la universidad no es mala idea.

Guillermo: Nosotros 4. _____ (estudiar) juntos [together] en la biblioteca. Si nosotros no 5. _____

(entender) algo, 6. _____ (poder) estudiar más. Los lunes, miércoles y viernes 7. _____ (almorzar) juntos en la cafetería. Los martes y jueves yo 8. _____ (almorzar) con mi novia.

Felipe: Yo 9. _____ (trabajar) todos los días, entonces [so] 10._____ (preferir) tomar clases por la noche.

Pablo: Yo 11. _____ (creer) que es una buena idea tomar clases por la noche.

Felipe: La universidad 12. _____ (costar) mucho dinero, y no sé si ahora mismo 13. _____ (poder) pagar tanto dinero [so much money].

Sebastián: Sí, es mucho dinero, pero vale la pena [it's worth it].

Felipe: Yo 14. _____ (jugar) al fútbol con mis amigos los sábados y domingos.

Sebastián: En la universidad también [also] 15. _____ (poder) jugar al fútbol.

Felipe: Voy a 16. _____ (pensar) en mis opciones [options], gracias. ¡Nos vemos!

Pablo, Guillermo, Sebastián: ¡Nos vemos

c. Escoge la preposición o el pronombre preposicional correcto para las oraciones siguientes. / Choose the correct preposition or prepositional pronoun for the following sentences.

ti mí   para   conmigo   contigo   de

detrás de   entre   hasta   sobre   con

1. Los lunes tengo clases _____ las nueve de la mañana y las cinco menos diez de la tarde.

2. En la clase hablamos _____ la situación política _____ Cuba.

3. Hablo _____ mis amigos todos los días.

4. ¿Quieres ir al seminario [seminar] de esta noche _____?

5. Esta tarea [homework] es _____ la clase de inglés.

6. Quiero ir a la fiesta, pero sin _____ no voy a ir.

7. Todos los días duermo _____ las ocho de la mañana.

8. Shhhh, la profesora está _____ nosotros.

d. Completa las respuestas de las siguientes preguntas. No olvides conjugar el verbo. / Complete the answers to the following questions. Don't forget to conjugate the verb.

1. ¿Juegas mucho al fútbol los fines de semana? No, _____ .

2. ¿Generalmente mientes a tus amigos? No, _____ .

3. ¿Pierdes las llaves [keys] de tu carro frecuentemente [frequently]? Sí, _____ .

4. ¿Cuánto cuesta un buen diccionario? _____ por lo menos [at least] veinte dólares.

5. ¿A qué hora almuerzas? _____ al mediodía.

6. ¿Entiendes los verbos con cambio de raíz en el presente? Sí,

_____

Respuestas correctas / Correct Answers

a. 1. chocolate   9. veintidós

2. hospital   10. almorzar

3. café   11. contigo

4. universidad   12. lecciones

5. palabra

6. Honduras

7. instrumento

8. ciudad

13. dormir

14. actividad

15. Málaga

b. 1. Prefiero

2. quiero

3. sabemos

4. estudiamos

5. entendemos

6. podemos

7. almorzamos

8. almuerzo

9. trabajo

10. prefiero

11. creo

12. cuesta

13. puedo

14. juego

15. puedes

16. pensar

c. 1. entre

2. sobre / de

3. con

4. conmigo

5. para

6. ti

7. hasta

8. detrás de

d. 1. No, no juego mucho al fútbol los fines de semana.

2. No, no miento a mis amigos.

3. Sí, pierdo las llaves de mi carro frecuentemente.

4. Un buen diccionario cuesta por lo menos veinte dólares.

5. Almuerzo al mediodía.

6. Sí, entiendo los verbos con cambio de raíz en el presente.

Ver, Dar, and Other Irregular Verbs

Vocabulario nuevo / New Vocabulary

maravilloso – marvelous **juntos** – together **exactamente** – exactly **enhorabuena** – congratulations **felicidades** – congratulations **la sierra** – mountain range, saw **la montaña** – mountain	**la Pascua** – Easter **la zona** – zone **la verdad** – truth **nevada** – snow-covered **colorado** – red-colored **florida** – covered with **flowers árido** – arid
siempre – always todos **a veces** – at times **de vez en cuando** – from time to time **a menudo** – often **frecuentemente** – frequently	**los días** – every day **tarde** – late **temprano** – early **el domingo** – on Sunday **los martes** – on Tuesdays
responder – to answer **ver** – to see **dar** – to give **escoger** – to choose **proteger** – to protect	**corregir** – to correct **decir** – to say, to tell **venir** – to come **oír** – to hear
la telenovela – soap opera **el presidente** – president **la situación** – situation **el líder** – leader **la reunión** – meeting	el **país** – country **la conversación** – conversation **la inmigración** – immigration **legal** – legal **ilegal** – illegal

Repaso general / General Review

U.S. State Names from Spanish

The five U.S. states with names that come directly from Spanish are Nevada, from nevada [snow-covered]; Colorado, from colorado [red-colored]; Montana, from montaña [mountain]; Florida, from florida [covered with flowers]; and California, from the fictional island of California that appears in the 16th-century Spanish book of chivalry entitled Las sergas de Esplandián [The Great Deeds of Esplandián].

Ver and dar

The verbs ver [to see] and dar [to give] both are irregular in the present. Ver has an extra e in the yo form and no accent in the vosotros form. The yo form of dar ends in -oy; the other five endings are the same as the regular -ar endings in the present, except there is no accent in the vosotros form. In the present, the six forms of dar rhyme with the six forms of ir. The conjugations of these two verbs in the present are as follows.

ver	[to see]	dar	[to give]
veo	vemos	doy	damos
ves	veis	das	dais
ve	ven	da	dan

Verbs like escoger

The verb escoger [to choose] has all regular endings in the present, but the yo form has a j instead of a g. If the yo form included a g, it would make a hard g sound, as found in tengo. To maintain the j sound present in escoger (and, for example, Argentina), the form instead is yo escojo. Other verbs conjugated like escoger include proteger [to protect] and the e à i stem-changing verb corregir [to correct]. The yo forms of these verbs in the present are yo protejo and yo corrijo.

Decir, venir, and oír

The present tense conjugations of decir [to say] and venir [to come] (which are both clearly -ir verbs) have two things in common: Both have a g in the yo form, and both are stem changing. Decir changes **e à i,** and venir changes **e à ie**, except in the yo form. The conjugations of these verbs in the present are as follows.

decir [to say]		venir [to come]	
e - i		e -ie	
digo	decimos	vengo	venimos
dices	decís	vienes	venís
dice	dicen	viene	vienen

Because venir is a verb of motion (like ir and llegar), it is often used with the preposition a (e.g., Siempre vengo a clase temprano is "I always come to class early").

When conjugated in the present, oír [to hear] has a g in the yo form; a y in the tú, usted, and ustedes forms; and an accent in the nosotros form. Its present tense conjugation is as follows.

oír [to hear]

oi**go**	o**ímos**
o**yes**	o**ís**
o**ye**	o**yen**

Improving Your Listening and Speaking Skills

Watching television in Spanish is one way to improve your listening and speaking skills. Specific networks that you might have access to where you live are Univisión, Telemundo, or Azteca. Although any program you watch can be useful, news programs are ideal for beginning language learners because newscasters tend to speak slowly and clearly. For someone new to the language, this is exactly the kind of spoken Spanish that you are most likely to understand. Moreover, when watching the news, you will see clips or scenes of what the newscaster is talking about. These images, accompanying what you hear, will help provide context for what you're hearing. When watching television, as always when hearing Spanish, use cognates, context, and conjecture to help you make sense of what you're hearing.

As has been mentioned in an earlier lesson, from time to time you should repeat what the newscaster is saying to work on developing your speaking skills. This will help you get accustomed to the intonation used in Spanish—meaning the way the voice rises and falls when speaking. And if you'd like to read subtitles while watching television, have them be in Spanish if possible. This entire all-Spanish experience—meaning that both the words you're hearing and the words you're reading are in Spanish—will help get you more accustomed to the language in its various aspects.

Actividades / Activities

a. Resuelve el siguiente crucigrama. / Solve the following crossword puzzle.

oír (2)   escoger   proteger   dar

venir   corregir   decir   ver

Horizontal / Across

2. Tú _____ las vacaciones suelen ser de diez minutos en una semana.

5. La profesora _____ los exámenes de sus estudiantes cada mes.

7. Ustedes _____ música cuando manejan su automóvil.

8. Yo siempre _____ la verdad (truth).

Vertical / Down

1. Los domingos vosotros _____ películas [movies] con vuestros amigos.

3. Mi hermano y yo siempre _____ lo mismo [the same thing] de la carta [menu] cuando vamos a un restaurante.

4. Yo _____ mi piel [skin] contra el sol todos los días.

6. Yo _____música cuando trabajo en la computadora.

8. Todos los años él le [to her] _____ un regalo [gift] a su mejor [best] amiga por su cumpleaños.

b. Erica y sus hijas Diana y Mariana están en la zoológico [zoo]. / Erica and her daughters Diana and Mariana are at the zoo.

Completa el diálogo con la conjugación correcta del verbo indicado. / Complete the dialogue with the correct

conjugation of the indicated verb.

Erica: Diana y Mariana, 1. ¿ _____ (oír) ese [that] sonido (sound)?

Diana: ¡Sí, mami!

Erica: Son las guacamayas [macaws]. ¡Están cantando! [They are singing]

Diana: ¿Por qué 2. _____ (cantar)?

Erica: Porque 3. _____ (estar) felices.

Erica: Diana, 4. _____ (ver) todos los colores [colors] de sus plumas [feathers]?

Diana: ¡Sí! ¿Por qué 5. _____ (tener) tantos [so many] colores?

Erica: Mmmm, porque 6. _____ (representar) [represent] los colores de la naturaleza [nature].

Erica: ¡Vamos a 7. _____ (ver) los monos [monkeys]!

Diana: No, mami! No 8. _____ (querer) ir.

Erica: ¿Por qué no 9. _____ (querer) ir? Tú siempre les [to them] 10. _____ (dar) comida [food] a los monos.

Diana: Hoy no quiero ver los monos.

Erica: Bueno, tú 11. _____ (deber) escoger qué animal quieres ver ahora.

Diana: Yo 12. _____ (querer) ver los elefantes [elephants].

Erica: Pero tú siempre 13. _____ (venir) a ver los elefantes. 14. _____ (ir) a ver otros animales ahora.

Diana: ¡No, mami! Es la primera vez que Mariana visita el zoológico y quiero 15. _____ (ver) los elefantes con ella.

Erica: ¿Los elefantes son tu animal favorito [favorite]?

Diana: No, mami. Yo no 16._____ (tener) un animal favorito. Todos 17. _____ (ser) muy bonitos.

c. Lee el siguiente párrafo y contesta las preguntas. / Read the following paragraph and answer the questions. Hoy, en la capital de los Estados Unidos, el presidente Obama se reunió con el presidente de México, Enrique Peña Nieto, para hablar de la situación económica de los dos países. Durante las conversaciones, los dos presidentes hablaron del Tratado de Libre Comercio de América del Norte y del asunto de la inmigración, tanto legal como ilegal, entre México y los Estados Unidos. Los dos líderes van a verse de nuevo en una semana cuando el presidente mexicano y el presidente estadounidense viajen a Río de Janeiro para una reunión de todos los jefes de Estado de las Américas.

1. ¿Cuándo van a verse [meet, see each other] de nuevo [again] los presidentes de los Estados Unidos y México? _____.

2. ¿Adónde van a viajar los presidentes? _____ .

3. ¿Por qué van a hacer el viaje [trip]?_____ .

4. ¿Quiénes más van a ser con los presidentes Peña Nieto y Obama?
_____ .

d. Lee el siguiente párrafo. Encuentra al menos cinco cognados y contesta las preguntas. / Read the following paragraph. Find at least five cognates and answer the questions.

El náhuatl

El náhuatl es una lengua que se habla principalmente en los pueblos indígenas nahuas en México. Aunque el náhuatl, con un millón y medio de hablantes en el país, es la lengua indígena hablada por el mayor número de grupos étnicos en México, también existe una gran cantidad de dialectos entre estos grupos. El náhuatl es la lengua indígena más importante en México, pero en ese país existen más de sesenta "lenguas vivas." Además de México, hay otros países que aún emplean lenguas prehispánicas como parte de su comunicación básica—por ejemplo, Guatemala, Ecuador, Perú y otros. El náhuatl y el español se han influenciado entre sí e incluso la Real Academia Española ha reconocido varios préstamos lingüísticos del náhuatl al español. Palabras como, por ejemplo, "chocolate," "tomate," "aguacate," "guacamole" y "tamal" son palabras en español que vienen de náhuatl.

Cognados: _____, _____,

_____,_____,

_____.

Cierto ("C") o Falso ("F") / True ("C") or False ("F")

1. Un millón y medio de personas hablan náhuatl en México.

_____

2. El español es la lengua indígena más importante de México.

_____

3. México es el único país que utiliza [uses] lenguas prehispánicas.

_____

4. La Real Academia Española no ha reconocido [has not recognized] los préstamos lingüísticos

[loanwords] del náhuatl. _____

Respuestas correctas / Correct Answers

a. 1. veis	6. oigo
2. vienes	7. oyen
3. escogemos	8. (horizontal) digo
4. protejo	8. (vertical) da
5. corrige	

b. 1. oyen / oís	10. das
2. cantan	11. debes

3. están   12. quiero

4. ves   13. vienes

5. tienen   14. Vamos

6. representan   15. ver

7. ver   16. tengo

8. quiero   17. son

9. quieres

c. 1. Van a verse de nuevo en una semana.

2. Van a viajar a Río de Janeiro.

3. Van a hacer el viaje porque hay una reunión de todos los jefes de Estado de las América.

4. Todos los jefes de Estado de las Américas van a estar con ellos.

Today, in the capital of the United States, President Obama met with the president of Mexico, Enrique Peña Nieto, to discuss the economic situation of the two countries. During the conversations, the two presidents discussed the North American Free Trade Agreement and the issue of immigration, both legal and illegal, between Mexico and the United States. The two leaders will meet again in a week when the Mexican president and U.S. president travel to Rio de Janeiro for a meeting of all heads of state of the Americas.

d. Cognados: millón [million], indígena [indigenous], número [number], grupos [groups], étnicos [ethnic], existe [exists], cantidad [quantity], dialectos [dialects], importantes [important], pre-hispánicas [pre-Hispanic], comunicación [communication], básica [basic], ejemplo [example], influenciado [influenced], reconocido [recognized], varios [various], chocolate [chocolate], tomate [tomato], tamal [tamale], guacamole [guacamole]

1. C.   2. F   3. F   4. F

The Present Progressive

Vocabulario nuevo / New Vocabulary

en este momento – at this moment **posible** – possible	**progresivo** – progressive
el tenis – tennis **la actividad** – activity **el tema** – topic **la comunidad** – community	**la felicidad** – happiness **la superioridad** – superiority **la cosa** – thing
ocurrir – to occur, to happen	**cambiar** – to change
el comedor – dining room **la comida** – food **la bebida** – drink **el plato** – plate **el tazón** – bowl	**el tenedor** – fork **el cuchillo** – knife **la cuchara** – spoon **la cucharita** – teaspoon
el platillo – saucer **la taza** – cup **el vaso** – glass **la copa** – wineglass, cocktail **el vino** – wine	**la servilleta** – napkin **el mantel** – tablecloth **la sal** – salt **la pimienta** – pepper **el azúcar** – sugar
el desayuno – breakfast **desayunar** – to eat breakfast **el almuerzo** – lunch	**almorzar** – to eat lunch **la cena** – dinner **cenar** – to eat dinner
la cafetería – cafeteria **la cocina** – kitchen **el cocinero** – male cook	**la cocinera** – female cook **el mesero** – waiter **la mesera** – waitress

Repaso general / General Review

The Present Progressive

The present progressive is a construction used to talk about something happening right now—something in progress at the moment the construction is being used. For that reason, it's often used with expressions like ahora [now], ahora mismo [right now], and en este momento [at this moment].

The construction consists of a form of estar in the present + present participle. To form the present participle, do the following: For an **-ar** verb, drop the **-ar** ending and add **-ando**; for an **-er** or **-ir** verb, drop the **-er** or **-ir** ending and add **-iendo** (e.g., bailar à bailando; aprender à aprendiendo; abrir à abriendo). An example of the present participle being used is **Estamos comiendo ahora**, which is "We are eating right now." [Note: The English sentence "Tomorrow

she is studying all day" is Mañana ella va a estudiar todo el día, using the **ir** + **a** + infinitive construction, because what's being described is not happening right now but, rather, will happen in the future.]

Verbs with Irregular Present Participles

There are two kinds of verbs with irregular present participles. One group of verbs with irregular present participles is -er and -ir verbs with stems that end in a vowel. Instead of an ending in -iendo, the participle for these verbs is -yendo with a y (e.g., leer à leyendo; oír à oyendo; traer à trayendo).

The second category of verbs with irregular present participles is the group of stem-changing -ir verbs. For -ir verbs with a stem-changing e, the e becomes i in the present participle. For -ir verbs with a stem-changing o, the o becomes u in the present participle (e.g., pedir à pidiendo; dormir à durmiendo).

Traits Common to Successful Language Learners

Every language learner is different, but quite often, successful language learners share common traits that help them as they progress with their studies. And if you can cultivate these traits as well, they will both help you improve your language skills more quickly and make it more likely that you remain dedicated to your studies. The three specific traits that characterize many successful language learners are urgency, belief, and selflessness.

Urgency doesn't mean that you should be racing through your lessons. It means, rather, both carrying on consistently with new lessons (interacting with the audio glossary, speaking activities, and workbook) and keeping in contact with the language even beyond the course as much as possible. This is particularly important at the stage you're at right now: halfway through the lessons. Quite often, the middle of a first course in Spanish is when language learners tend to become frustrated, give up, and stop studying. This happens because although they've learned a fair amount, learners realize that what they don't know is much greater than what they do know. This can lead some learners to become frustrated with their progress. But a sense of urgency helps fight feelings of frustration. So, move through these lessons as consistently and diligently as you reasonably can, and work to find ways to use Spanish beyond the class as well.

The second trait that characterizes successful beginning language learners is belief—meaning maintaining faith that the language-learning process really works and that it will work for you. Quite often, the learners who progress the most in their language studies are those who truly believe that with time, practice, and consistent contact with the language, their Spanish skills will indeed improve significantly.

The third trait shared by many successful language learners is selflessness. Clearly, you made the decision to study Spanish, and you are the one taking this course. But very often when a learner gains proficiency in Spanish, other people benefit as well. Maybe your language skills will help you do your job better; perhaps there are people in your community you'll be able to help when you're bilingual. Whatever the case, be aware that your continued study of the language has positive effects beyond you. And remembering these benefits to others might serve as a good motivation to continue your studies.

Actividades / Activities

a. Todos los días Cecilia ve la nueva telenovela La oveja negra, pero hoy tiene que trabajar hasta tarde en un proyecto muy importante. Ella llama a su amiga Alejandra para que ella le cuente lo que está pasando en la historia. / Every day Cecilia watches the new soap opera The Black Sheep, but today she has to work late on a very important project. She calls her friend Alejandra so that she can tell her what's happening in the story.

Completa las frases siguientes usando el presente progresivo. / Complete the following sentences using the present progressive.

Cecilia: Hola, Alejandra. ¿Qué estás haciendo ahora?

Alejandra: Hola, Cecilia. 1. _____ 2. _____ (ver) La oveja negra.

Alejandra: ¿Y tú? ¿Qué estás haciendo? ¿No 3. _____ 4. _____ (mirar) la novela?

Cecilia: No, no puedo porque 5. _____ 6. _____ (trabajar) en la oficina. Tengo un proyecto muy importante que hacer. Mi asistente [assistant] y yo 7. _____.

8. _____ (escribir) los objetivos [objectives] del proyecto ahora mismo. Alejandra: ¡Oh, no! ¡Qué terrible! Cecilia: ¡Lo sé! Por favor, ¿puedes decirme lo que 9. _____ 10. _____ (ocurrir) en la novela? Alejandra: ¡Claro! La

novela 11._____ 12. _____ (empezar) en este momento. Ángel Ernesto 13. _____ 14. _____ (hablar) con el cantinero [bartender]. Él está muy confundido porque él quiere a Antonieta María, pero él 15. _____ 16. _____ (pensar) que también quiere a Adela Lucero. Cecilia: Pero Adela Lucero no quiere a Ángel Ernesto, ¿cierto? Alejandra: No estoy segura [sure]. Ahora, Adela Lucero 17. _____ 18. _____ (leer) y 19. _____ 20. _____ (romper [to rip up]) las cartas [letters] de Ángel Ernesto. Cecilia: ¿Qué 21. _____ 22. _____ (ocurrir) con María Esmeralda y Lucero? Alejandra: Ellas 23. _____ 24. _____ (llorar [to cry]) porque ahora Adela Lucero 25. _____ 26. _____ (empacar [to pack]) para ir a trabajar en otra ciudad. ¡Oh, noooo! Cecilia: ¿Qué pasa? Alejandra: Antonieta María 27. _____ 28. _____ (quemar [to burn]) las cartas de Ángel Ernesto. Yo 29. _____ 30. _____ (pensar) que ella sabe sobre Adela. ¡Y ahora, parece que Ángel Ernesto 31. _____ 32. _____ (caminar) hacia la casa de Adela! Cecilia: ¿Y Enrique Alonso? Él es el novio de Adela, ¿verdad? Alejandra: Sí, él es su novio. ¡En estos momentos, él 33. _____ 34. _____ (manejar) su carro hacia la casa de Adela! Cecilia y Alejandra: ¡Ooohhh!

b. Hoy hay un partido de fútbol importante, entonces Erica, Javier y sus hijas están visitando a los padres de Erica para ver juntos el partido. / Today there is an important soccer game, so Erica, Javier, and their daughters are visiting Erica's parents to see the game together.

Completa las frases siguientes usando el presente progresivo. / Complete the following sentences using the present progressive.

Diana: Mami, estoy aburrida. ¿Quieres jugar conmigo?

Erica: No puedo, mi amor [love]. Yo 1. _____ 2. _____ (dormir) a tu hermanita. Puedes jugar con tu abuelito.

Diana: No, mami, abuelito 3. _____ 4. _____ (cocinar) la carne [meat] en la parrilla [grill].

Erica: ¿Y abuelita?

Diana: Ella 5. _____ 6. _____ (servir) la comida.

Erica: ¿Y tu tío Felipe?

Diana: Tío Felipe y tía Elena 7. _____ 8. _____ (mirar) otro partido de fútbol.

Erica: ¿Y tu papá?

Diana: Papi 9. _____ 10. _____ (oír) las noticias [news].

Erica: ¿Y tu amigo Sebastián?

Diana: Él 11. _____ 12. _____ (jugar) al
fútbol con su papá. Y yo no quiero jugar porque hace mucho calor.

Erica: Niña, ¿qué estoy haciendo contigo en los últimos diez minutos?

Diana: ¡Sí! Gracias, mami.

c. Completa las siguientes respuestas con el presente progresivo del
verbo indicado. / Complete the following answers with the present
progressive of the indicated verb.

1. ¿Qué estás haciendo en este momento? _____ (hacer) los ejercicios
en el cuaderno del curso.

2. ¿Qué está haciendo tu mascota [pet] ahora? _____ (dormir) en el
suelo [floor].

3. ¿Qué están haciendo tus amigos en este momento? _____ (leer) el
periódico.

Lectura cultural / Cultural Reading

Lee el texto siguiente y contesta las preguntas de forma cierto ("C") o
falso ("F"). / Read the following text and answer the questions as
either true ("C") or false ("F").

El tuk-tuk o mototaxi como medio de transporte

Entre los medios de transporte tradicionales, encontramos alrededor del mundo trenes, autobuses, taxis, bicicletas, carros, barcos o aviones. Otro de estos medios muy populares especialmente en Asia es el tuk-tuk, el cual es una versión del rickshaw, o carro de dos ruedas jalado por una persona. La diferencia entre el rickshaw y el tuk-tuk es que este último es un triciclo con motor que se usa cada vez más en otros países del mundo, incluyendo algunos en América Latina.

Este triciclo es muy popular para el transporte de personas, especialmente en lugares con muchos turistas. Los países que lo utilizan incluyen China, India, Tailandia, Indonesia y algunos países de Europa, como Italia y Holanda. En Centroamérica, hay versiones del tuk-tuk en El Salvador, Guatemala, Honduras y Nicaragua. Actualmente, en Cuba se utiliza como taxi sobre todo en La Habana, en donde les llaman "coco taxi" porque parece ser una fruta del coco sobre un scooter. En América del Sur, también tienen este medio de transporte, por ejemplo, en Ecuador, Perú y Colombia. En Colombia, lo llaman "motocarro," y es utilizado en ciudades pequeñas.

Aunque este vehículo motorizado de tres ruedas no es tan rápido como los carros convencionales, es bastante conveniente por dos razones: usa poca gasolina y produce poca contaminación del medio ambiente. De hecho, actualmente hay compañías en los Estados Unidos interesadas en producir un modelo de tuk-tuk eléctrico.

1. El tuk-tuk es muy popular en Asia. _____

2. El rickshaw es un triciclo con motor. _____

3. El tuk-tuk es un carro de dos ruedas jalado por una persona.
_____

4. Todos los países de Centroamérica utilizan [use] el tuk-tuk.
_____

5. Una ventaja [advantage] del tuk-tuk es que no usa mucha gasolina.
_____

Respuestas correctas / Correct Answers

a. 1. Estoy	18. leyendo
2. viendo	19. está
3. estás	20. rompiendo
4. mirando	21. está
5. estoy	22. ocurriendo
6. trabajando	23. están
7. estamos	24. llorando
8. escribiendo	25. está
9. está	26. empacando
10. ocurriendo	27. está
11. está	28. quemando
12. empezando	29. estoy
13. está	30. pensando

14. hablando	31. está
15. está	32. caminando
16. pensando	33. está
17. está	34. manejando
b. 1. estoy	7. están
2. durmiendo	8. mirando
3. está	9. está
4. cocinando	10. oyendo
5. está	11. está
6. sirviendo	12. jugando

c. 1. Estoy haciendo	3. Están leyendo
2. Está durmiendo	

Lectura cultural

1. C   2. F   3. F   4. F   5. C

The Tuk-Tuk or Motortaxi as a Means of Transportation

Traditional means of transportation we find around the world include trains, buses, taxis, bicycles, cars, boats, and airplanes. Another of these popular means of transportation, especially in Asia, is the tuk-tuk, which is a version of the rickshaw, a two-wheeled car pulled by a person. The difference between the rickshaw and the tuk-tuk is that the tuktuk is a motorized tricycle that's used more and more in other countries of the world, including some in Latin America.

This tricycle is very popular for the transport of people, especially in places with many tourists. Countries that use it include China, India, Thailand, Indonesia, and some European countries, such as Italy and Holland. In Central America, there are versions of the tuk-tuk in El Salvador, Guatemala, Honduras, and Nicaragua. Nowadays, in Cuba it's used mostly as a taxi in Havana, where they are called "coco taxi" ["coco" means "coconut"] because it seems to be a coconut on top of a scooter. In South America, they also have this means of transportation in, for example, Ecuador, Peru, and Colombia. In Colombia, it's called "motocarro" and is used in small cities.

Although this three-wheeled motorized vehicle is not as fast as conventional cars, it's rather convenient for two reasons: It doesn't use much gasoline, and it doesn't pollute the environment very much. In fact, there are now companies in the United States that are interested in producing an electric tuk-tuk model.

Direct Object Pronouns and Adverbs

Vocabulario nuevo / New Vocabulary

me – me **te** – you [informal, singular] **lo** – him, it [masculine, singular] **la** – her, it [feminine, singular]	**nos** – us **os** – you [informal, plural] **los** – them [masculine] **las** – them [feminine]
el tipo – kind, type **el objeto directo** – direct object	**el dinero** – money
el té – tea **el jugo de naranja** – orange juice **la leche** – milk **el pan** – bread **el pan tostado** – toast	**la mantequilla** – butter **la mermelada** – jam **el cereal** – cereal **los huevos** – eggs **el tocino** – bacon
tostar – to toast **hacer un brindis** – to make a toast	**funcionar** – to work, to function
el refresco – soft drink **la cerveza** – beer **el sándwich** – sandwich **la sopa** – soup **el jamón** – ham **el pavo** – turkey **el queso** – cheese	**la pasta** – pasta **los frijoles** – beans **el arroz** – rice **la papa** – potato **la fruta** – fruit **el postre** – dessert **salado** – salty
bastante – rather, quite **despacio** – slowly **probablemente** – probably **a lo mejor** – maybe	**cierto** – certain **claro** – clear **todavía** – still

bien – well	**afortunadamente** – fortunately
mal – poorly	**inmediatamente** – immediately
como – like,as	
así – so, like this	**actualmente** – at present
demasiado – too much	**realmente** – actually
cuidadoso – careful	

Repaso general / General Review

Direct Object Pronouns

The direct object receives the action of the verb and answers the question "what?" or "whom?" with relation to the verb. You have seen direct objects in an earlier lesson when you learned about the a personal (e.g., abuelos is the direct object in Vemos a nuestros abuelos, which is "We see our grandparents"). Direct object pronouns are used to replace direct object nouns to avoid redundancy.

The direct object pronoun always goes before a conjugated verb (e.g., "My brothers look at me" is Mis hermanos me miran; "I look at them" is Los miro). If there's a no in the sentence, the no goes before the pronoun (e.g., No te creo is "I don't believe you"). When using a direct object pronoun, the a personal is never used.

The eight direct object pronouns are as follows.

me	nos
te	os

lo   los

la   las

Direct Object Pronouns Used with Nonconjugated Verbs

You have already learned that direct object pronouns must go before a conjugated verb. However, in the case of a nonconjugated verb (e.g., an infinitive or a present participle), the direct object pronoun can go either before the conjugated verb, where it usually goes, or after and attached to the infinitive or the present participle (e.g., Lo voy a hacer and Voy a hacerlo both mean "I'm going to do it"; Las estamos lavando and Estamos lavándolas both mean "We are washing them"). When adding direct object pronouns to either infinitives or present participles, you might need to add an accent to maintain the original stress (as in lavándolas, which maintains the stress on the syllable van, which is where the word is stressed in Las estamos lavando).

Adverbs

Adverbs are used to modify verbs, adjectives, or other adverbs; as a result, adverbs have only one form. Unlike adjectives (which agree in number and gender with the noun modified), adverbs do not change based on the word they are modifying. There are some words that can be used either as an adjective or an adverb. In these cases, the word must agree with the noun modified when it's used as an adjective but is unvariable when it's used as an adverb (e.g., using poco as an adjective: Hay pocas mujeres aquí is "There are few women here"; using poco as an adverb: Las chicas leen poco is "The girls don't read much").

One way to form an adverb is to add the suffix -mente to the feminine singular form of an adjective (e.g., activa + -mente à activamente [actively]; general + -mente à generalmente [generally]). When two adverbs are used in the same sentence, only the second needs the suffix -mente (e.g., El hombre canta fuerte y terriblemente is "The man sings loudly and terribly"). A common way to make an adverbial expression is to use the preposition con before a noun (e.g., con frecuencia is frequently; con cuidado is carefully).

Actividades / Activities

a. El Dr. Esteban Quirós tiene una paciente que está muy enojada porque se siente mal todos los días. Ella dice que todos los días está cansada y que nunca tiene energía. / Dr. Esteban Quirós has a patient who is very angry because she feels bad every day. She says that every day she's tired and never has any energy.

En el siguiente diálogo, reemplaza los objetos directos subrayados con los pronombres apropiados. / In the following dialogue, replace the underlined direct objects with the appropriate pronouns.

Dr. Quirós: ¿Usted come comida saludable [healthy]?

Paciente: No, no 1. _____ como.

Dr. Quirós: ¿Usted ve muchos programas de televisión [television programs]?

Paciente: Sí, claro 2. _____ veo hasta muy tarde en la noche.

Dr. Quirós: ¿Usted toma pastillas [pills] para dormir?

Paciente: Sí, 3. _____ tomo todas las noches.

Dr. Quirós: ¿Usted toma otros medicamentos [medicines]?

Paciente: Sí, tomo vitaminas [vitamins] todos los días. Pero 4. _____ tomo en la mañana.

Dr. Quirós: ¿Usted hace ejercicio?

Paciente: No, nunca [never] 5. _____ hago. Tampoco [Neither] veo deportes [sports].

Dr. Quirós: ¿Usted fuma [smoke] cigarrillos [cigarrettes]?

Paciente: Sí, 6. _____ fumo, pero solo cuando estoy estresada [stressed].

Dr. Quirós: ¿Y cuándo está estresada?

Paciente: Todos los días. Pero doctor, yo me siento [I feel] mal y tengo demasiado trabajo. Nunca tengo energía y estoy muy cansada. Pero yo tomo vitaminas todos los días.

Dr. Quirós: Sí, entiendo que 7. _____ toma, pero usted fuma, no come comida saludable, no hace ejercicio, está siempre estresada y duerme pocas horas. ¡Tiene que tener mucho más cuidado con su salud!

b. ¡Hace muy buen tiempo! Elena y sus amigas Rebeca y Alicia van a hacer un picnic en el parque. Ellas necesitan saber si tienen toda la comida que necesitan. / The weather is great! Elena and her friends Rebeca and Alicia are going to have a picnic in the park. They need to know if they have all the food they need.

Reemplaza los objetos directos subrayados con los pronombres apropiados. / Replace the underlined direct objects with the appropriate pronouns.

Elena: Rebeca, ¿tienes el café? Sí, 1. _____ tengo, pero no tengo el pan.

Alicia: Yo 2. _____ tengo.

Rebeca: ¿Elena, tienes la mantequilla y la mermelada?

Elena: Sí, 3. _____ tengo. ¿Tú tienes el jugo de naranja?

Rebeca: Sí, 4. _____ tengo, pero yo no quiero jugo de naranja. Yo quiero café con leche. ¿Tienes leche en el refrigerador [refrigerator], Elena?

Alicia: No, no está en el refrigerador porque yo 5. _____ tengo aquí.

Elena: Muy bien, gracias. ¿Tienes los huevos, Alicia?

Alicia: 6. Sí, _____ estoy preparando ahora mismo.

c. Javier quiere hacer una reunión de amigos de la secundaria en su casa. Él está pidiéndoles ayuda a todos para hacer la reunión. / Javier wants to have a gathering of friends from high school at his home. He is asking everyone to help with the gathering.

Escoge la respuesta correcta con el pronombre de objeto directo apropiado. / Choose the correct answer with the appropriate direct object pronoun.

1. Ingrid: ¿Puedes llamar a Patricia y Virginia?

a) Sí, puedo llamarnos mañana.

b) Sí, puedo llamarlas mañana.

c) Sí, puedo llamarlos mañana.

2. Ingrid: Javier, ¿cuándo vas a limpiar tu casa?

a) Voy a limpiarlo el sábado.

b) Voy a limpiarme el sábado.

c) Voy a limpiarla el sábado.

3. Ingrid: ¿Necesitas ayuda para limpiar tu casa?

a) No, no la necesito, gracias.

b) No, no me necesito, gracias.

c) No, no nos necesito, gracias.

4. Javier: Ingrid, ¿me llamas más tarde? Quiero saber si Patricia y Virginia pueden venir.

a) ¡Sí, claro! Te voy a llamar en la noche.

b) ¡Sí, claro! Me voy a llamar en la noche.

c) ¡Sí, claro! Nos voy a llamar en la noche.

5. Vania: Javier, ¿vas a invitar a Manrique y Antonio?

a) Sí, posiblemente os voy a invitar ahora.

b) Sí, posiblemente te voy a invitar ahora.

c) Sí, posiblemente los voy a invitar ahora.

6. Javier: Vania, ¿quieres tú hacer un brindis en la reunión?

a) No, yo no quiero hacerme.

b) No, yo no quiero hacerlo.

c) No, yo no quiero hacerlos.

7. Néstor: ¿Quién va a comprar las cervezas, Javier?

a) Yo. Las voy a comprar después.

b) Yo. Los voy a comprar después.

c) Yo. Me voy a comprar después.

8. Javier: Vania, ¿puedes preparar el postre? Tú cocinas muy bien.

a) ¡Sí, por supuesto! Yo me puedo preparar.

b) ¡Sí, por supuesto! Yo os puedo preparar.

c) ¡Sí, por supuesto! Yo lo puedo preparar.

d. Elena, Rebeca y Alicia están hablando. / Elena, Rebeca, and Alicia are talking.

Completa las frases con los adverbios apropiados. / Complete the sentences with the appropriate adverbs.

| temprano | mucho t | ambién (2) | aquí | claro |
| ahora | bastante | posiblemente | | poco |

Alicia: Creo que hace tiempo perfecto [perfect] hoy.

Rebeca: Yo 1. _____ lo creo.

Alicia: ¡Qué lugar [place] tan [so] bonito! Este parque es 2. _____ tranquilo.

Elena: Sí, por eso [that's why] 3. _____ hay muchos niños. Son las ocho de la mañana, es 4. _____, pero 5. _____ en la tarde van a venir más niños.

Rebeca: ¿Vamos a estudiar juntas para el examen del lunes?

Alicia: Sí, 6. ¡_____! Pero yo voy a estudiar solo un 7. _____. Estoy muy cansada.

Elena: Yo necesito estudiar 8. _____. Tengo miedo de ese examen.

Rebeca: Yo 9. _____ tengo miedo. ¿Podemos empezar a estudiar 10. _____, no?

Elena: ¡Buena idea!

Alicia: ¡Es hora de estudiar!

Respuestas correctas / Correct Answers

a. 1. la   5. lo

2. los   6. los

3. las   7. las

4. las

b. 1. lo   4. lo

2. lo   5. la

3. las   6. los

c. 1. b   5. c

2. c   6. b

3. a   7. a

4. a   8. c

d. 1. también   6. claro

2. bastante   7. poco

3. aquí   8. mucho

4. temprano   9. también

5. posiblemente   10. ahora

Next Steps in Improving Your Spanish

Vocabulario nuevo / New Vocabulary

la profesión – profession	**la tecnología** – technology
el maestro – teacher **el abogado** – lawyer **el hombre de negocios** – businessman **la mujer de negocios** – businesswoman **el arquitecto** – architect	**el enfermero** – nurse **el director** de escuela – school principal **el trabajador social** – social worker **el policía** – police officer
el sitio web – website **la página web** – web page **el blog** – blog **el correo electrónico** – e-mail **el mensaje de texto** – text message	**el usuario** – user **el enlace** – link **la conexión** – connection **el buscador** – search engine
chatear – to chat online **acceder a Internet** – to access the Internet **descargar** – to download **navegar por la red** – to surf the Internet **el nombre de usuario** – username **Trato de leer mucho.** – I try to read a lot.	**la contraseña** – password **el/la Internet** – Internet **la conexión inalámbrica** – wireless connection **el teléfono inalámbrico** – cordless phone **el teléfono celular/el celular/el móvil** – cell phone **animar** – to encourage

Repaso general / General Review

Verbs Followed by a Preposition

You have already learned several verbs that are followed by a preposition: asistir a is "to attend"; salir de is "to leave"; jugar a is "to play a sport." Other verbs that are followed by a preposition include tratar (which is followed by de) and entrar (which is follwed by a or en). Siempre trato de estudiar antes de un examen is "I always try to study before an exam." As for entrar, Latin Americans tend to follow it with a, while Spaniards tend to follow it with en. So, to say "At times we enter the building late," a Latin American would say A veces entramos al edificio tarde, and a Spaniard would say A veces entramos en el edificio tarde.

Verbs That Need a Preposition before an Infinitive

You've learned in general that in Spanish, if you place one verb directly after another, the first verb is the one that is conjugated, and the second verb needs to be in the infinitive form (e.g., Ellos quieren navegar por la red is "They want to surf the Internet"; No puedes hablar conmigo ahora is "You can't talk to me now").

But there are some verbs that must be followed by a preposition before an infinitive. Two examples of this you've seen already are acabar de [to have just done something] and ir a [to be going to do something] (e.g., Elena acaba de dormir is "Elena just slept"; Vamos a chatear is

"We are going to chat online"). Four other verbs that need a preposition before an infinitive (and specifically the preposition a) are empezar [to begin], comenzar [to begin], aprender [to learn], and enseñar [to teach]. Consider these examples: Es hora de empezar a trabajar is "It's time to begin to work"; Al mediodía, los abogados empiezan a llegar al restaurante is "At noon, the lawyers begin arriving at the restaurant"; Pedro debe aprender a manejar is "Pedro should learn to drive"; Su hermano lo enseñó a mentir is "His brother taught him to lie").

Immersing Yourself in Spanish

One good way to improve your Spanish is to force yourself to speak it. So, if you have someone you can speak Spanish with, meet and decide that you will speak only Spanish for an hour, a dinner, or a certain event—you decide. Of course, more time is better, but no matter how much time you spend speaking Spanish, the important thing is to continue with it. The impossibility of using English really forces you to try to (tratar de) figure out how to express yourself in Spanish. And your companion doesn't need to be a native speaker; he or she could be another Spanish language learner like you.

Know that when you have difficulties expressing yourself, it's okay. Often, a problem in communication will lead a learner to study a bit more—maybe grammar, maybe vocabulary. But the learner tends to be motivated because the studying is designed to solve a real communication problem that occurred during the immersive experience.

The Learning Curve of a Language Learner

Sometimes language learners imagine that their progress in studying a language will be a steadily ascending curve, starting with a baseline knowledge of zero and gradually but steadily moving upward toward communicative competence. The reality, however, is that while the progress of a language learner has many ups, it also has some downs. And there are definitely periods when your skills plateau and you seem not to be improving at all.

So, you need to know that it's entirely normal—to be expected, even—that there will be times when you feel stuck, and you think that you've stopped improving or even gotten worse with your Spanish skills. When this happens, don't give up. Continue your studies and keep in contact with the language as much as possible. The more you hear, speak, read, and write Spanish, the more quickly you'll notice that your Spanish really is getting better.

Actividades / Activities

a. Lee el párrafo y contesta las preguntas que siguen. / Read the
paragraph and answer the questions that follow.

Luisa está planeando [planning] una reunión de vecinos. Ella quiere
hacer la reunión en su casa. Además, quiere ver a sus nietas Diana y
Mariana, y por eso también invitó a la reunión a su hija Erica y a su
yerno Javier. Ella envió [sent] un correo electrónico la semana pasada,
pero no todos enviaron una respuesta. Luisa va a mandarles otro
mensaje a sus vecinos. La reunión va a ser mañana a las 6:30 de la
tarde. Luisa quiere hablarles mañana sobre la necesidad [need] de tener
un servicio de policía privado [private] en el vecindario. Ella también
está preocupada porque últimamente [lately] alrededor del vecindario
hay mucha basura [trash]. Algunos de los vecinos le dijeron a Luisa
que estos son asuntos [issues] importantes de discutir [discuss]. Ella
les dijo a todos que pueden llevar sus iPads para tomar notas [notes], y
además [moreover] todos pueden usar su conexión inalámbrica. Luisa
está enviándole un mensaje de texto a su hija para recordarle sobre la
reunión.

1. ¿Cuáles son dos expresiones que hablan de acciones en el futuro?

_____ .

2. ¿Cuáles son tres verbos conjugados en el pretérito? _____ .

3. ¿Cuál es un ejemplo del uso del presente progresivo (que expresa
algo que ocurre ahora mismo)? _____ .

4. ¿Cuáles son tres ejemplos del uso del objeto indirecto? _____.

5. ¿Cuál es un uso de estar para expresar una emoción? _____ .

b. Completa las oraciones usando el pretérito. / Complete the sentences using the preterite.

Cuando Diego 1. _____ (empezar) su compañía [company], 2. _____ (pedir) un servicio de Internet con conexión inalámbrica. Él 3. _____ (comprar) una computadora, un teléfono celular y otro inalámbrico. Al principio, 4. _____ (tener) problemas para acceder a Internet y la conexión no 5. _____ (ser) la mejor, y por eso 6. _____ (llamar) a la compañía de Internet para solicitar [ask for] una conexión más rápida. En la compañía, ellos le 7. _____ (ayudar), y Diego 8. _____ (obtener) [to get] una mejor conexión. Cuando él 9. _____ (cerrar) su empresa, 10. _____ (vender) todas las cosas de su oficina.

c. Escoge la opción correcta. / Choose the correct answer.

1. Luisa _____ un blog para hablar de nutrición desde hace cinco años.

a) tuvo b) va a tener c) tiene

2. En este momento, Luisa y Esteban _____ tener una página web con información sobre medicina y nutrición.

a) quisieron b) van a querer c) quieren

3. Luisa _____ a todos los vecinos del vecindario, y por eso la reunión va a ser en su casa.

a) conoció b) va a conocer c) conoce

4. Elena y su esposo _____ a la reunión de mañana.

a) fueron b) van a ir c) van

5. Alejandra _____ directora de escuela por unos años, antes de casarse [to get married].

a) fue b) va a ser c) es

6. A Alejandra le gusta mucho su nuevo teléfono celular y todos los días _____ mensajes de texto.

a) mandó b) van a mandar c) manda

7. El primer año de universidad, Pablo _____ en estudiar enfermería [nursing], pero ahora no _____ estudiar enfermería.

a) pensó…quiere b) van a pensar…quiso c) piensa…quiere

8. Ahora tú _____ dos correos electrónicos.

a) tuviste b) vas a tener c) tienes

9. Ayer, tú y tus amigos _____ en el mejor restaurante de la ciudad.

a) comieron b) van a comer c) comen

10. Tus amigos y tu _____ muchos correos electrónicos ayer durante el trabajo.

a) enviaron b) van a enviar c) envían

Lectura cultural / Cultural reading

El cacao

El árbol del cacao es originario de América, probablemente de los Andes. La planta del cacao es una planta tropical que requiere un clima caliente y constantes lluvias. La cosecha de esta fruta puede obtenerse durante varios meses del año, y en algunos países ocurre en cualquier momento. Esta fruta es la base para lo que conocemos como chocolate y también para el mole, por ejemplo, una salsa que es una especialidad de Puebla, México. Parece que los productos derivados del cacao se consumían mucho tiempo antes de la llegada de los españoles al Nuevo Mundo, incluyendo bebidas fermentadas. Además de sus usos gastronómicos, antes de 1492 se utilizaba el grano del cacao como moneda en Mesoamérica.

Hay muchas variedades de la planta de cacao, pero en general, la planta tiene altos niveles de antioxidantes que pueden ayudar a combatir el envejecimiento y ayudar con los problemas cardiovasculares. A pesar de ser un producto originario de América, hoy en día los principales productores del cacao, con 70% de la producción mundial, son los países en África del Oeste, incluyendo Costa de Marfil, Camerún y Ghana. En Asia se cultiva la planta en Indonesia y Malasia, mientras que en las Américas hay cacao en Colombia, Ecuador, Brasil, México y la República Dominicana. Para muchos pequeños agricultores y comerciantes, el cacao representa una fuente de ingresos importante.

Aunque Nicaragua no es uno de los principales países productores del cacao en el mundo, tiene proyectos de cultivo, comercialización y exportación que han originado grandes beneficios para la población nicaragüense. En Matagalpa se produce uno de los mejores cafés de Nicaragua, pero los pequeños agricultores de la ciudad han encontrado en la producción del cacao otra oportunidad de tener una mejor rentabilidad e ingresos en sus cultivos. Gracias al cacao, algunos nicaragüenses han encontrado respuestas a sus problemas económicos que no habían podido solucionar solo con el cultivo del café.

1. ¿Qué requiere la planta del cacao? _____.

2. ¿Cuáles son tres principales países productores de cacao?

_____.

3. ¿Quiénes producen el 70% de la producción mundial del cacao?

_____.

4. ¿Dónde se produce uno de los mejores cafés de Nicaragua?

_____.

Respuestas correctas / Correct Answers

a. 1. va a mandarles / va a ser

2. invitó / envió / enviaron / dijeron / dijo

3. está planeando / está enviándole

4. va a mandarles / quiere hablarles / le dijeron / les dijo / está enviándole / recordarle

5. está preocupada

b. 1. empezó   6. llamó

2. pidió   7. ayudaron

3. compró   8. obtuvo

4. tuvo   9. cerró

5. fue   10. vendió

c. 1. c) tiene   6. c) manda

2. c) quieren   7. a) pensó…quiere

3. c) conoce   8. b) vas a tener / c) tienes

4. b) van a ir / c) van   9. a) comieron

5. a) fue   10. a) enviaron

Lectura cultural

1. Requiere un clima caliente y constantes lluvias.

2. Entre otros, Costa de Marfil, Camerún y Ghana son principales países productores de cacao.

3. Los países de África del Oeste.

4. En la ciudad de Matagalpa.

Cocoa

The cacao tree is native to the Americas, probably from the Andes. The cocoa plant is a tropical plant that requires a hot climate and constant rains. The harvesting of this fruit can be done during various months of the year, and in some countries it occurs at any time. This fruit is the basis for what we know as chocolate and also for mole, for example, a sauce that is a specialty of Puebla, Mexico. It seems that the products derived from cocoa were being consumed long before the arrival of the Spaniards in the New World, including fermented beverages. In addition to its gastronomic uses, before 1492 the cocoa bean was used as currency in Mesoamerica.

There are many varieties of the cocoa plant, but in general the plant has high levels of antioxidants that can help to fight aging and help with cardiovascular problems. Despite being a product originating in America, nowadays the principal producers of cocoa, with 70% of worldwide production, are the countries of West Africa, including Ivory Coast,Cameroon, and Ghana. In Asia, the plant is cultivated in Indonesia and Malaysia, while in the Americas there is cocoa in Colombia, Ecuador, Brazil, Mexico, and the Dominican Republc. For many small farmers and businesspeople, cocoa represents an important source of income.

Although Nicaragua is not one of the main cocoa-producing countries in the world, it has projects of cultivation, commercialization, and export that have produced great benefits for the Nicarguan people. One of Nicaragua's best coffees is produced in Matagalpa, but the small farmers of the city have found in the production of cocoa another opportunity to have better profitability and revenues in their farming. Thanks to cocoa, some Nicaraguans have found answers to their economic problems that they had not been able to solve by only growing coffee beans.

Disclaimer

Disclaimer All the material contained in this book is provided for educational and informational purposes only. No responsibility can be taken for any results or outcomes resulting from the use of this material. While every attempt has been made to provide information that is both accurate and effective, the author does not assume any responsibility for the accuracy or use/misuse of this information.

CPSIA information can be obtained
at www.ICGtesting.com
Printed in the USA
LVHW081253160320
650166LV00008B/51